James Roberts is a writer and artist who lives in the hills of the Welsh Border country. His essays and poems have been published widely and his artwork has featured in several exhibitions, books and theatre productions. This is his first book of non-fiction.

seariverwood.com

@seariverwood

TWO LIGHTS

Walking at Dawn and Dusk on a Turning Planet

-

JAMES ROBERTS

september

This paperback edition published in the United Kingdom by September in 2025
First published in the United Kingdom by September Publishing in 2024

September, an imprint of Duckworth Books Ltd
1 Golden Court, Richmond, TW9 1EU, United Kingdom
www.septemberpublishing.org

A catalogue record for this book is available from the British Library

Typeset by RefineCatch Limited, www.refinecatch.com

Printed and bound in Great Britain by Clays Ltd, Elcograf S.p.A.

The authorised representative in the EEA is
Easy Access System Europe, Mustamäe tee 50, 10621 Tallinn, Estonia

Paperback ISBN: 9781914613739
eISBN: 9781912836918

MIX
Paper | Supporting responsible forestry
FSC® C018072

CONTENTS

For Julia, and the wolf

CHASING THE DAWN

The dawn begins with seabirds, with the first faint wash of rose-tinted light touching their feathers. There are crested auklets perched on lava flows and sea cliffs. They are here in their millions. The sounds they make, as their milk-pale eyes open, creak and grate, as if overnight the salt winds have penetrated their workings. In among them are tufted puffins, red-legged kittiwakes, short-tailed albatrosses. Their purrs and shrieks begin.

But no, I have the sequence wrong. Before the seabirds felt the first glow of today out on the Bering Sea, already a soft light had touched the peaks of the Koryaksky volcano further east, where a pair of golden eagles sat on a broken crag, their eyes burning amber. A split second before the first auks began their rusting chorus the female fell into the air, spread her wings and pierced the rock with her screams.

There is a line separating day and night that travels continuously around the world. It is a perfect wave of light which triggers a wave of sound. The line of dawn is also the line of dusk. It crosses Chennai and Moscow at the same time. White-throated kingfishers wake and open their beaks synchronised perfectly with the first calls of great northern divers. Green bee-eaters and jungle babblers time their songs with ptarmigans and Arctic terns.

And already I'm lost, trying to imagine something so complex as a wave of light and sound sliding across a continent. I can't imagine how the dawn penetrates a boreal forest like this one marked on the map, surrounding a place called Zhigansk in the East Siberian taiga. Does the light skim the tops of the trees first and do the birds perched high in their branches start to sing minutes before those lower down, who are still muffled in last night's darkness? Or does one call fire and begin a fusillade of calls, ricocheting through the forest as the light trickles into it in a million places, running down pine needles, leaves and polished bark, the calls of hawk owls, Siberian jays, golden mountain thrushes, rosefinches and red-flanked bluetails? There are other birds whose names I'll never know, more sensitive to the changing light, whose calls are as soft as breath and only carry the length of a branch.

A map is such a crude creation. I'm looking at a double-page spread which contains the whole of Russia and because I've been educated to think that our mark-makings are important I start to think I know something about a place I'll never see, smell, touch or hear. My focus is drawn by a green area on the northern coast, punctuated by hundreds of blue dots, all of them lakes, tiny to my eyes, little pools. But this is a view seen as if from a satellite, miles above Earth, so each of them must be huge. I wonder how the dawn arrives in a place like this. At home the swifts and cuckoos have returned, last of the migrants. Perhaps some birds are still on their way to Siberia, which is so much further north. The lakes I'm looking at are covered with thawing ice, cracked and splintered like smashed glass, containing a deep translucent blue, the colour of a mind empty of thought, starting to glow beneath the first tendrils of light. Millions of broken mirrors begin to reflect space. In the places where the ice has cleared tundra swans are uncurling their necks from the feathered warmth of their wings. Ross's gulls begin to twitch as the first snow bunting, out on the tundra, calls. A wintry chorus begins, low and mournful, full of loneliness, a beckoning to the birds still on their way, beyond the horizon, and the species long gone, but still present somehow. Frozen in the permafrost are the bodies of extinct birds, found occasionally in the summer thaw, like the perfectly preserved body of a crested lark which was discovered recently, along with the remains of a woolly rhinoceros.

Light is penetrating the lands to the south. People are already awake, tending to animals, preparing for a long day of work. The freezing wind bends the grasses and the thin light arcs along each blade. A citrine wagtail, heading north to Siberia, flicks into life and emits two thin peeps, drowned in the hiss of the wind. Then a call I know well, but don't hear enough, rises out of the distance like a sunset in sound. Eurasian curlews are breeding here. Many other birds familiar to our northerly island are also resident. There are skylarks, buntings, sparrows, magpies and crows, their calls familiar along a band of Earth stretching five thousand miles. Among them are steppe eagles, saker and Amur falcons, their high-pitched screams scissoring through the chorus.

On the Mongolian steppe a father is breathing heavily, plumes of steam coming from his mouth as he climbs a slope of scree towards a line of quickthorn trees which have just appeared out of the darkness and now hover in front of a rock wall. He reaches the trees and quickly plucks twenty long thorns from their branches. A little further away is a birch that he will cut a piece of bark from with his knife. Beneath the bark he will prise a piece of sapwood and carve it roughly into the shape of a boat. Then he will hurry home with the light turning purple and pink amid the first calls of harlequin ducks and bean geese, which he will ignore as he thinks only about his sick boy whose bed he will sow with the thorns. Just before sunrise he will suspend the boat over the child's head to carry off the sickness.

Frost is melting on the sand dunes of the Gobi Desert. Far to the south the light is coming up fast over tropical beaches fringed with trees. A pink-headed fruit dove has just opened its eyes and uttered a soft, almost inaudible *hoo*, seconds before the low-high pipe of a Javan sunbird. The sea is flat calm out to the horizon. In front of it a temple complex is as still as the cliffs. Then, suddenly, the sound of drums, which makes the bird flee its perch and retreat up the mountain as a line of people, dressed in white shirts and bright sarongs, round the corner of the rock and climb the steep path.

They carry tall flags of every colour and pattern which taper into the sky. They all bear flowers which they scatter as they walk. They cross the rocks and disappear one by one into the water temple, the last of them entering as the first burning line of the sun appears. All the islands of Indonesia are now illuminated. Here the chorus is short and loud, a brass band of birds with beaks as spectacular as their feathers. In the trees there are hornbills and barbets, flowerpeckers and honeyeaters, on the water pelicans, darters, stone-curlews, stilts.

The band of light is speeding. It pours from Jakarta to Medan in minutes and is already crossing the Bay of Bengal. Soon Kolkata, Chennai and Colombo will roar into life. The band has already passed over several mega-cities, places permanently illuminated, where songbirds call all night and the dawn chorus is drowned in machine noise. Even when the sun has risen above the horizon, no one sees until it is overhead, staring down like a blind eye. Most of the birds here are silent. Their corpses are being shipped, crammed into boxes, between abattoirs, warehouses and markets. In the fume-scented parks songbirds are singing in remembrance of the green places that still lie beneath the roads and pavements, the piped rivers and buried streams.

An hour ago the human ripple began with fishermen talking in low voices as they put out their nets. Now their song has gathered into a million waves. Small children are chattering to their toys while parents drink tea and whisper about bad dreams that are only just starting to fade. Sons and daughters are listening to the last words of dying parents while nurses softly mutter instructions to each other. Lovers are quarrelling or moaning with joy. Farmers and herdsmen are talking to their animals. Street cleaners and night workers, coming home, stop to exchange words about the cold, about their aches and pains. Old people are rocking with sorrow, staring out of windows at landscapes they no longer recognise. Athletes are motivating themselves with words that somehow pour energy into their aching muscles. Field workers and factory workers are cursing the way their lives took a bad turn and swearing that things will be different, or that things will never change. Torturers are dismissing their acts of the previous day. Singers are clearing their throats, expanding their airways, tuning up. Some songs are being sung for the first time, some for the last. Words from old languages are being uttered before going extinct. Most of the voices in most of the places are coming out of screens, listened to by a billion starers. A few people, not nearly enough, are sitting quietly, listening to birds.

There are huge areas, the size of countries, where the light has washed in in silence. The continent-crossing forests that once teemed with multiple symphonies of birds are now islands with ever-withdrawing coastlines. They are surrounded by ordered seas of farmland or encroached on by green deserts. Dawn spreads quickly in these places, a uniform line of light that shows a single wash of colour, hand-chosen by us. Every time the wave of light crosses Earth, more of the wild has been lost. Dawn diffuses in plumes of smoke rising from forest fires, gets mirrored back into the sky off polished metal and glass, pale concrete. The edge of the rising sun glints off masts, wires and turbines where there were trees only weeks before. It is seen high above Earth, long before it touches the ground, by people in planes staring from windows at the curvature of Earth while they travel between identical places.

The dawn calls that were once a choir of voices endlessly building now follow multiple and thinning threads, some of them broken. The sound passes along the edges of rivers and streams, down steep ravines, across scrubby plains, over sheer ridges where trees cling to shelves of rock, across bog and marsh, disused railway lines, city parks and corridors, along the edges of multilane highways and over green bridges. Calls diffuse and concentrate. A taper of corvid cries travels along a wire for a hundred miles then runs into a pool of life, opening into a multitude of song where the old concentrations of life still hold. This pool is a zoo.

*

I wake in the dark, sit up and light a small lamp. Its reach is limited. In a big room you can almost see the globe it makes, how the light curves back into the dark. There was a year in my life when I had no access to electricity and my night-time light came from this lamp. Once I crossed a field in the early hours, holding it up, and almost walked into a hippopotamus. Only the reflected glint in the corner of the creature's eye warned me it was there.

The universe is a place of permanent night lit by lanterns like mine, globes of light illuminating the surfaces of other globes as they spin and oscillate. On Mercury the dawn lasts a full Earth day and never reaches its poles at any time of the solar year. The time between one sunrise and the next is 176 days. On Venus there are only two dawns in the whole of its solar year. Jupiter rotates so fast that its storm-wracked dawns occur 10,476 times each year. The poles of Uranus point directly at the sun giving each of them forty-two years of day, forty-two years of night and a single, long, freezing dawn in between. Due to its gaseous composition and speed of rotation, days on Uranus are twisted out of shape. At the poles they last twelve hours, at the equator eighteen. If eyes were on its surface to witness, the dawn would be shrouded in clouds being hurled across its skies at supersonic speeds.

*

The light has reached the great barrier of the Alps and is touching the ice of its highest peaks, which are starting to glow. Alpine swifts have been on the wing all night and remain silent until the sun is up, which they will see first of all creatures. A chough nods and grates its first call. Light is crossing the peak of Hochtor, and Zirbitzkogel, minutes later Birkkarspitze and Wildspitze, bringing salutations from rock ptarmigans and black grouses. It touches the knife-edge peak of Finsteraarhorn, then on to Täschhorn, Dom and Monte Rosa amid the cries of bearded vultures. It touches Pic de Rochebrune, Arcalod, Mont Blanc. It has taken 50 minutes to cross the 750 miles of the Alps from east to west. It travels across the lowlands of France, silhouetting the shapes of empty castles and ruins where doves shelter in alcoves. It travels down motorways and picks out the rectangles of warehouses, floods thousands of acres of monocrops. It touches the spires of old cathedrals kindling the blazing cries of peregrine falcons. It weaves into dense woodlands and forests, silencing owls and nightjars and beckoning forth the tick-tick songs of wrens. It picks out the wings of wind turbines and the feathered corpses that lie on the ground beneath them. It crosses Picardy and Normandy and finally touches the sea again. Black-backed gulls and herring gulls are raucous.

*

Finally, it reaches my island home and fifteen minutes later I am up, fog-eyed, preparing tea. I walk into the garden, shivering a little. It is 4 a.m. I am facing east. Above me the last stars are fading out of an indigo sky. On the horizon is a band of burnt orange, graduating to turquoise. Strands of cloud hang like tail feathers. A bat is circling the house and on its second lap it comes so low over my head that my cheeks feel the air its wings displace. Still silence. Then the first bird calls, a blackbird perched in my neighbour's ash tree. Then another blackbird calling back from a stand of oaks. A pheasant croaks in the field and a robin starts piping, a thin chorus of four still so quiet I can hear the bat's wingbeats. For minutes it continues like this while the light changes colour and the field edges come into view across the valley. A crow calls, and another. A pigeon coos softly. Then the finches and tits start to sing. A wren, a jay. The blackbird has hopped from the tree on to my neighbour's roof and now it is singing loud. My foggy mind is trying to detect its patterns and repetitions but a blackbird's song has endless variations. The air is changing, a sudden plume of cold, a whisper of wind and on it more birdsong carries, further off, from the trees and hedges, the old millpond, the river. The rooks are awake. Only a couple, calling to each other nearby. Then four rise into the sky. They swerve, turn and land again. It wakes the rookery down in the valley and now all I can hear are rooks, perhaps two hundred of them, like a brass section out of tune with the rest of the orchestra. An orange curtain rises for the day to begin. The stars have vanished. The world is a theatre of birdsong.

We live on the side of a high ridge that runs from the Herefordshire border into Wales. It overlooks the Black Mountains to the south and the Cambrian Mountains to the north. To the west are the peaks of the Brecon Beacons. They're all green peaks, flat-topped with fingered ridges. Between the ridges are deeply carved valleys threaded with rivers and streams. Scattered along the valleys are hamlets and villages, little towns. Narrow lanes spider away from them, up steep slopes to the small farms which have been here for many generations. Apart from in the valley bottoms, where the climate is warmer and the soil more fertile, this landscape is dominated by sheep and cattle farming. The towns each have their livestock market, social hubs for the scattered population. The surrounding hilltops are mostly common land, dominated by bracken, bilberry and heather, perfect habitats for ground-nesting birds.

It was perhaps a search for natural richness that led my family to this place. We moved when our first son was a few months

old, thinking that we might be able to give him a *Swallows and Amazons* childhood. The uplands are huge, open spaces. From the summits of the hills the views are spectacular. The light play, on the many days of rain and broken cloud, is mesmerising, the topography sculpted with creases and folds, crests and waves. It's a brooding landscape which inspires the imagination. These hills are storied, mythical places, scattered with old earthworks, sunken lanes, standing stones, cairns and barrows. The skies are filled with circling buzzards and red kites.

I was in my mid-twenties before I encountered a landscape that teemed with wildlife. I was brought up in the suburbs of Stoke-on-Trent, in a house that overlooked the winding gear of the local coal mine. It was a city made up of huge constellations of identical housing estates spread around a still-functioning industrial centre dominated by coal and clay. I only have three memories about the wildlife in that place. I remember the bodies of dead hedgehogs that began to appear in the playing field across the road from our house one year, so many of them that we kids created a hedgehog graveyard in the boggy ground at the edge of the cricket pitch. I remember a friend at primary school who used to go nesting. He had boxes filled with strangely coloured and patterned eggs, and a shed at the back of his house where he kept a kestrel in a cage. And I remember the tawny owl which sat on the telephone pole at eye level to my bedroom window every night for a whole winter. These memories are burned into me when most of my childhood is now a fading blur. I believe that a fascination with wild creatures exists in all children. It's a species-deep connection, an unbroken thread that has stayed with us for hundreds of millennia, going back to when we woke at dawn in places which sang with a multitude of voices. It's a connection that most of us now forget as we reach puberty and adulthood.

The first mountain I ever walked up was Great Gable in the Lake District. We hiked it in the worst possible weather, the March wind, snow and sleet battering us all the way to the summit, which we had to crawl to. We were working-class city kids with no experience and no equipment. I remember scrambling up a slope of scree near the summit. When we got over the ledge at the top there were sheep peering down at us, disinterested, as if this mountain were no mountain at all. What I remember most is how the place changed as the rain came down, how waterfalls appeared and started foaming into the valleys, how the stream which we were camped next to became a torrent, rising metres in a few hours, washing our tents away. It was freezing cold, dark, dangerous. And beautiful. I'd like to say that this experience led me back to the uplands frequently, but it didn't, though the place left a deep impression on me. The uplands became a question that recurred once in a while, but a decade passed before I went back there. Perhaps I'd intuited that the wildness I'd experienced in that place was also an emptiness, that it sang of loss.

For years after that hike I only spent time in cities, Wolverhampton and Birmingham, then London. I studied design at polytechnic, then worked a job in computer graphics for several years before getting the urge to travel. In my mid-twenties I took a flight to Tangier and crossed Africa, most of the time spent in the Congo, Uganda and Kenya. It was on a sleeper train from Kampala to Nairobi that I first encountered a truly wild place. I opened the cabin curtains at dawn to see a plain stretching to the horizon, filled with animals. There were zebras and antelopes, circling hawks, troops of baboons, rhinos, serval cats. We passed the huge corpse of a giraffe, its ribs splayed like hands in prayer, cloaked with flies, pecked at by white-backed vultures. In the distance the parched grasses were pooled with dark, shifting blurs, herds of wildebeest on the move. Between the herds there were grazing cattle watched over by red-clad tribesmen. That scene became an ideal for me, a community that encompassed and stretched beyond the human village, humming with life.

I don't know when my thoughts began to be shaped by birds. Once I rescued a stranded blackbird chick, housed it in a shoe box in the side porch of my parents' house and fed it bread and milk for three days. When I went to it on the fourth day it was tipped forwards into its feeding bowl, its head bent to the side, its eyes shut. When it was alive it gawped and pecked at me. When it was dead I stroked its downy lizard body, its bony beak.

Forty years later I tried to rescue a rook chick which possibly didn't need my help. It had attempted to fly from the nest too early and was sitting in the lane, screeching to its parents, which, as far as I could tell, were not responding. I took it back to the house, found a shoe box and was about to repeat the mistake I'd made as a child before my wife Julia told me I needed to put the bird outside, as close to the nest as possible, so that its parents could find it. I followed that advice and in three days found its dead body draped in a hedge. The wild is always out of reach.

I've never been overly interested in the science of birds, in the machinery of them, and I have a stack of unread books to prove it. I'm not much of a birdwatcher and I can't identify many of the rarer species even after years of trying. I'm an artist and what I love about birds is their artistry, the shapes they make with the light, their music, their constant transformations. Today a buzzard floated over my head so low I could almost touch it. I saw every bar on its feathers, its amber eye, its sickle talons. I froze for a second, watched it pass, tried to hold on to its form so I could draw it later. But it slipped away. Tonight it could die in the storm that is blowing in. Or it could pair and breed in the woods that overlook my house, watching me from a distance all summer.

Behind our house, only a few metres from the bedroom wall, is a huge copper beech tree. Its branches are draped over our heads, its roots splayed under our feet. In spring it's an all-day sunset, filled with birds. A rookery is slowly being built in the tree, only four nests at the moment. All day I can hear the rooks' calls, their footsteps and beak taps on the roof only centimetres from my head. At night they are silent except for the occasional cackle and squawk, a response, perhaps, to something experienced in a corvid dream. I'm not sure how long it takes for a rookery to become established, but I'm hoping soon for a winter dusk where hundreds of them shoal above my head, shrieking and sparring, flipping upside down, bringing the space above the house into ecstatic life.

*

Most artists are obsessed with space. Positive space is the area of a picture which contains the subject, the details, the face or figure in a portrait, the arranged objects in a still life, the trees and rocks in a landscape. Negative space is the area of the picture which surrounds the subject. My favourite paintings are by masters of both. I've spent hours staring at Vermeer's *Woman in Blue Reading a Letter*, wondering how he managed to achieve the milky light in the room, the sense of silence, the open-mouthed expression on the pregnant woman's face and the depths behind it. Patrick Heron achieved something similar in his abstract painting *Blue Painting – Venetian Disc and Black Column*, a picture which sings colour, which your eyes can dance with. In recent years I've become fascinated with ancient Chinese mountain landscape paintings and the poems which often accompany them. These are masterworks of negative space, the artists coming from a philosophical tradition which recognised and celebrated the emptiness from which all things emanate. Mountains appear from the mist, then disappear back into it, the way all of the ten thousand things do.

In the uplands the landscape and its inhabitants dissolve frequently. Negative space dominates. This phenomenon has become the inspiration for my visual imagination. I paint the silhouettes of distant mountains, the outlines of cliffs squalled featureless by rain, birds in flight. When I draw I use ink, salt and water, the simplest method I can find. With one drop of ink, one of water and a few grains of salt you can create an image which reflects the fluidity of life. The salt interacts to create unpredictable textures, like threads of water across sand, like phosphorescent sparks, like storm clouds. It's the unpredictability that I love and the speed with which the shapes and textures materialise, as if by themselves. Occasionally an image emerges which has some of the life of the place or bird, some of its movement, its fleetingness. The best images seem to be appearing and disappearing simultaneously, the way an owl does, caught briefly in the light from a window, or a goshawk in the daytime dusk beneath the canopy of a wood.

*

Twilight is the time of day I love most. Forms dissolve, accompanied by the slow quieting of the earth. The land shape-shifts. There is an out breath, particularly in places like this where most living things are inhabitants of the light. Dusk is the best time to be in the uplands. It allows you to come to your senses. There's a joy in watching a well-known track disappear ahead of you, for the outlines in the land to fade back and transform. I follow the tracks made by animal footprints across the hill, which are sometimes distinct, deep furrows trampled through high bracken; and sometimes faint, just a slight indentation in the moss. At dusk they slowly blend with the terrain as if a comb has smoothed them out. In the valley below the hedges begin to erase, the scissored lines of the fields blur, barns and farmhouses sink into the dark. The trees seem to hold their forms longest, bleeding an inky stain which lingers into night. There's a hypnotising quality to this transformation. In some of the bleakest times of my life I've gone to the hills at dusk just so I can breathe, walking to an out-of-the-way spot overlooking the valley and mountains beyond. There I can find the place inside me that watches, that point of attention beyond the tangled ruminations, observing the transience of things. As the place fades back to its essence, shedding the scars, so do I.

At dusk the hills become pure source, their silhouettes starting points for flares of life. Trees at the edge of a pool are the beginnings of a forest stretching all the way to the sea. The peaks of the whaleback mountains are foothills beyond which towers of ice-covered rock climb. Across the moor the wolves are hunting. I sit with my back to the trunk of an oak where an eagle owl perches, staring down with orange eyes. Earth imagines continually, sculpts new forms, erases them, sculpts again. This is the cycle inside which all other cycles turn.

Twilight is the simplest of phenomena, yet the transformation it brings about reveals life at its most complex, different in every place, at every time. The line of dawn passes over almost nine million eukaryotic species each day, 80 per cent of them we have yet to discover, and has passed over billions more which are now extinct. At dusk a wave of fish and invertebrates rise from the depths of the oceans in such densities that they shut out the last of the solar light, replacing it with their own luminescence as they hunt and try to conceal themselves from hunters. In many places, however, silences, and not songs, are more often audible.

There was once a temperate rainforest here, covering most of these hills. It was removed and replaced by a farming system which provided habitat for a hugely reduced number of species, but the uplands still thrummed with life. Now industrial agriculture has taken over, part of the great acceleration. Only small areas remain which still contain their original riches, the places we've abandoned or find too inconvenient to farm or fish: steep ravines and little commons filled with trees; estuaries and wetlands which are still home to large populations of waders and wintering geese; offshore islands where abandoned fields are burrowed by nesting seabirds. These are the places I love most, the landscapes of life. Over the years they've tuned me into the wild, recreated the bond that we all feel ultimately.

Wherever I go I try to find the hidden places where wild creatures gather. Yesterday I drove to a valley I'd never been to before to see a little wild river winding out of the high hills. When I got out of the car the place was silent except for the tumbling of the water. An hour later I still hadn't seen or heard a bird. I moved on, followed the mountain road to the sea and then turned north, where I stopped again at a miles-long beach bordering an estuary. There, in front of the dunes and an ancient drowned forest, I sat and watched a hundred sandpipers feeding at the edge of the tide, rushing forwards and backwards with the sliding water, spooking to rise in an echelon, out over the dunes. It was worth the journey.

In the uplands places rich with life can be hard to find, but they're there if you know where to look.

There's a bare place on the hill where a stream has cut its way east down a steep slope into a flooded area of sedge and star moss. It's a roosting site for golden plovers from October to April. They gather there in little groups through the autumn until the flock has grown to around two hundred birds. The plovers are so still, so silent and well camouflaged on the ground that a walker can be almost in the middle of them before spotting them. I've happened on the flock many times in shifting mist, at first noticing only that the ground in front of me seems to be quivering, then sliding, the birds moving away from me in a wave, before a single call sounds the alarm and the birds rise in a rush. They flee over the other side of the ridge for a moment, then return and circle overhead, sometimes high up, at other times almost skimming the ground. As they change direction they flash silver-white, the flock moving as a single, convulsing organism. The dead zone of the hill comes back to life. The weight in me lessens. I'm light as a bird. I can fly.

WAITING FOR COMETS, WATCHING FOR SWANS

There is a camera mounted on the side of a shining spacecraft which is orbiting Earth, peering down on a storm, a whorl the shape of a thumbprint, the size of a country. We can see every detail, its white centre pitted with little craters, like a microscope's view of human skin. Light pours out of it, a luminescent pool lifting into space, as if the storm clouds were a source, not a reflector. It is a dazzlingly bright scene, utterly peaceful. The camera shifts position and shows the spacecraft's foiled instrumentation, its solar wings sparkling with the whiteness of the storm below. It changes position again, slowly, almost frustratingly serene. Only minutes ago the spacecraft glided above the line of dawn, a perfect shallow arc stretching across the planet, on one side the blue speckled night, on the other the incendiary day. Below, Earth is turning so fast it feels that if someone were to step down on to it they would slip and fall off. The arms and legs of coastal peninsulas are traceries filled in by a tattooist's needle. The rolling continents are over-scrawled with a dense zebra patterning of high cloud. Forty minutes pass and it is night again. The moon has not risen and the stars are bright, though not as bright as the orange-yellow lights three hundred miles below, cityscapes intersected with grids and radial lines. In places they connect one to the other, electric amoeba engulfing forests, pushing long tentacles into valleys, over hills and mountains. For a time the craft passes over a vast plain with little signs of human presence. Then a burst of lightning turns into a sequence of flares as multiple electrical storms connect in the distance. They flicker as if coded communication is passing between them. The camera rotates again and this time reveals the line of Earth's atmosphere, a thin band like the edge of a mist that could be blown away with a breath. It's not the grandeur of our planet you see from space, but its fragility. The band starts to fade. Dawn is about to appear for the sixteenth time today. It will not be the hour-hand-slow transformation we earthbound viewers witness, but a dazzling, rapid procession. Already the edge of the world has turned white. Just above this blazing line the comet appears, huge and plummeting, a firework heading into deep space, its split tail trailing thousands of miles behind it. A fantastic bird.

*

The swans are in the big field next to the river, a hundred of them at least. This morning I stood watching while most of them slept curled into their wings, sitting in the thinly sown grass. Since then they've flown in groups only a few feet from the surface of the water and then turned to bank above the broken skeletons of the willows, before returning to their roosting places. Or they've spent the whole day plodding slowly across the field grazing weeds, or not moving at all, lost in sleep. Now they're over at the far side of the field, half a mile off, close to the road. Though I can't see them I can see the ghosts of their shapes, little pale patches, distant constellations. Or maybe I'm imagining it. They're as silent as stars. I'll never comprehend that silence. Are swans the least vocal of birds? They're so enigmatic that even their necks create a question mark. When I was a boy I was instructed that all swans are dangerous. A single wingbeat could break a limb. When I passed the only pair I knew, who nested in a tree that had fallen into the old mill pond across the field from our house, they hissed and snaked out their necks at me. I saw their jet-black eyes, their webbed, scaly feet, the cold insides of their beaks, and shivered. It's strange how we can change the shapes of things in our minds, or make shapes from nothing.

There must be thin cloud in the sky tonight because I can't see any stars, only the winking red and blue lights of jets as they head north along the edge of Europe before crossing the Atlantic, following Earth's curve for thousands of miles. I've only once been on a transatlantic flight. What I remember is looking down at the tip of Greenland and seeing fractal patterns of icebergs floating in the blue, as still and as white as swans. Whiteness has a mesmeric quality to the human eye. We stare at frozen summits, watch as snow descends. When I was at art school, a teacher made me pin a white sheet of paper to a wall and then spend three days painting it. I thought it was a prank, until I started seeing the colours passing across its surface. Now I know that whiteness can hold every colour and take the shapes of all that we project on to it, even here, at dusk, when the light is almost extinguished. The swans draw me in like a mystery. Their familiarity disguises an otherness. They're here and far away. I watch them long after they've disappeared into the dark.

It's hard to identify the instant when twilight becomes night. The sunlight that has drained away completely somehow leaves a tail of luminescence which attaches to objects in the landscape, petals, stones, swans. At this time of day, the imagination projects its own light on to the things we think are there, but are not. I see owls skirting the field, badgers snuffling the earth. There are voles at the water's edge, weasels and stoats, and a pair of foxes are stitching the hedges with their coats the colour of sunset. But can we trust our eyes? Isn't the imagination always projecting? I've possibly witnessed this scene in a painting, a film or a book. Most likely I've invented it, with a little help from the twilight. In reality the field in front of me is empty right to the river's edge, apart from the group of sleeping swans. It has been recently poisoned with weed-killing chemicals, then ploughed and planted with rapeseed, which will be factory-processed into fuel. For most of the year this place is devoid of life. But this is the countryside and here, perhaps more than anywhere else, we populate the place with ghosts. The swans, however, are real and I'm lucky to be watching them now, learning from their stillness and silence. When they're around I know that the evolutionary work of art that this planet embodies is still extant, and very much in progress.

I'm scanning the horizon with binoculars, using a compass to detect the position of a star. I've found a spot at the top of the hill, facing the Cambrian Mountains. But the sky is still too pale to see stars in the north, though in the south many are visible. An hour ago Antares appeared above the Black Mountains. Now it has rolled higher and I can see the Scorpius constellation it is the centre of. Overhead is Draco and Ursa Minor; Gamma Draconis, Gemma; Deneb, Sadr, the Cygnus constellation. But to the north a glowing corona of turquoise twilight lingers, edged with burnt orange, though it is only an hour until midnight.

I'm hoping to get a glimpse of the comet Neowise, which should be just above the northern horizon, below the star Capella. I cannot see Capella. Perhaps this high hill isn't high enough. It doesn't matter, it's a perfect night, one of those rarities here when there is little cloud and no wind. I have an unobstructed view of the whole dome of the sky, while the earth below has disappeared, all its details, the clotted edges of woods, the intersecting hedges, tracks and lanes. Gone for now. This area is known for its dark skies, being one of the least populated places in the country. There is nothing in front of me for fifty miles except bare hills, deep valleys and lonely farms. I climb up on to the roof of the car and stare at the day as it retreats, trying to feel the turning of the planet. At this latitude Earth is rotating at approximately six hundred miles per hour. It's orbiting the sun at a thousand times that speed. Stars, trillions of miles apart, are rolling in and out of view, crossing the sky in hours.

I seem to miss so much of the present, letting my internal gaze wander elsewhere, almost anywhere. Even now, with this perfect view of the retreating twilight, on this perfect night, I'm finding it hard to focus on the place in the sky where the comet is supposed to be. I'm losing concentration, starting to dream. I put the binoculars aside and lie back, looking straight up at Cygnus, trying to picture the long neck and wide wings of a swan.

*

There is a pool on the hill which is a point of focus for most walkers. From the highest point of the ridge, on a day when the sun spears down through gaps in the cloud, the oval of water glows with the whitest light. I must have spent a thousand hours watching it. The pool is usually empty of birds by December, but last winter it was inhabited by a single juvenile swan. Its parents arrived early that March, circling over the passage flocks of teal and mallards. Within a week they began to build their nest in a hidden place beneath high reeds. Six eggs hatched in early May. Swans are the most vigilant parents and for the following period the tiny cygnets were guided around the pool by their parents, travelling in single file with the pen leading and cob guarding. The cygnets doubled in size every few weeks.

By early July the cob had let down his guard a little and had begun to wander away from the family, while the cygnets travelled in a cluster, following the pen, but not too closely. One morning the cob was gone.

The moult began in late summer, feathers rimming the pool. The cygnets were by now almost the size of the pen, though they still followed her everywhere. Their infant voices remained, the continual shy *seep* that seemed incongruous with their size. A few weeks later, with the ends of the bracken fronds curled and brown, the pen began flying lessons, spreading and beating her wings and launching herself across the pool. The cygnets reared out of the water, agitating their own wings, but were still unable to fly. On a late September morning I arrived just after dawn to see the pen and only four cygnets. A few days later, there were two. Then, on a day when the first mist blurred the whole valley, I looked over a silver oval of water now empty of swans. I walked down to the nest. Then I heard the call of a cygnet and looked up to see it bending and poking among the reeds.

Winter arrived early. The pool became a cobweb of ice. Crunching across the frost one morning, before the sun had come up, I saw the silhouette of the swan out in the middle. Its head was drooping unnaturally, its beak close to the surface. I watched it for a while and it didn't look up. I could see dark patches at the top of its neck. I called the vet and he came in waders and managed to pick his way across the ice to the bird. It struggled as he lifted it, but soon gave up. Later in the day I went to visit the surgery and the vet showed me to a computer screen where he pulled up an X-ray of the bird. Dotted around the skull and upper vertebrae was a bright constellation of ten silver stars, pellets from an air rifle. The swan had been euthanised.

I imagine it would have been a casual act for the person who shot the bird. Perhaps it was feeding, its slim head snaking in and out of the water, a challenging target. Count it slowly, the way I imagine the shooter would have done, closing one eye, setting up, taking aim, pausing to adjust position. One … two … three … four … five … six … seven … eight … nine … ten. Perhaps a minute or more passed between each shot, the bird unable to move from its tiny puddle of water surrounded by ice, too stunned after the first shot to attempt an escape. The shooter would have put the gun back on their shoulder, stamped their feet to get them warm again, watched the swan list a little, its neck droop. They would have shaken their head in disbelief that the bird was still alive. Or perhaps they were a little disappointed by the strange calm of the creature. They would have looked down into the water, at their reflection, seen someone staring back, amplified and distorted by the fractured lens of ice. Then they would have casually walked away.

This event made me wake up to what I was witnessing in the hills surrounding my home, something I'd been in denial about for years because of the beauty of the terrain. The commons are not wild places but part of a tradition where life is closely controlled and sometimes not tolerated. The long spines of the valleys are bitten back, shaved bare, deeply scarred. It is their losses which define them.

Healthy communities reach out beyond the household and the

village, into the fields and woods, along the streams and rivers, up into the hills and mountains. They're communities of place, not just of people, of multiple species living intertwined. Ted Hughes, in one of his letters, stated that he thought all children are in mourning for the natural world. When I first read this statement I didn't quite understand or agree with it. Now I feel that we are all in mourning. An advancing loneliness has taken hold of us. For almost all of our existence, encompassing half a million years, we humans have been surrounded by a myriad of sibling species. Now we are living in a time when some of us will never witness a truly wild place and its inhabitants.

Our human footprint has become huge, displacing or eradicating much of what was left of the wild. The creatures we once wove into our songs and stories, even into our names, are hidden from us. Extinctions are happening at an accelerating rate. In Wales our skies are no longer home to turtle doves and corn buntings. Red squirrels and water voles are on the edge, along with over a thousand other species.

I was almost forty years old when I saw my first curlew and I was overwhelmed when I heard its call, which I thought and still think is the most beautiful of natural sounds. Occasionally I've woken to it when a lone bird has flown over the house at dawn. On every occasion I've burst into tears, but I cry when witnessing beauty much more than when I'm sad. For me, in those trailing notes is the wonder of the world. When I first heard that sound I didn't know about their decline. I wish I still didn't.

I have a sheet of paper in a drawer in my desk on which is

written the area bird recorder's curlew count going back decades. Every year since the record began shows a loss from the previous year, from hundreds of pairs down to only a handful. If it was mapped as a linear graph it would look like the steep-sided profile of a glacier-carved ridge. Many of the species which were once abundant here show similar declines. These declines, in this tiny area of a tiny country, follow a pattern which radiates across the globe and has now affected every place I've ever been to, most of the losses happening in the fifty years of my lifetime. I've come to look at this period as a descent into half-light.

The poet Jim Harrison wrote that he was often overwhelmed by the beauty of places, but, most of all, by not being able to see them as they should be. It's a statement which is now on constant replay for me. Everywhere I go, every walk I take in these hills, I'm reminded of the swan and all the other beings which have been erased from this place.

*

There's a line from one of my favourite poems by W. S. Merwin which repeats in my head constantly: 'All day the stars watch from long ago'. It's the first line from 'Rain Light', one of the finest poems I know. That line stretches time in a way it's almost impossible to do with just eight words. It speaks of the vast distances of the universe, of hidden beauty and of those who are gone, but who can see, somehow, through our eyes. Perhaps they're our ancestors, perhaps our gods. It's a line that works on me in times of suffering, when I feel like there's no end to it. At those times I become so inhabited by the loops, rewinds and playbacks of my thoughts it's almost impossible to see that there's a universe out there, miraculous from edge to edge. I've just come through such a time, a three-year period which I thought would never end. It began with the death of my father, an agonisingly slow process at the end of a decades-long decline caused by Parkinson's disease. A few months later an old friend died. Another funeral followed. At the same time my eldest son spiralled down into a dangerous depression which had Julia and I frantic with worry that he too would not survive. Months followed of lurching fear every time he went out of the house or when his room went quiet. Then, just as he recovered, Julia was diagnosed with breast cancer.

It's so hard to see in times of loss, so hard to know the stars are watching. A twilight descends on us. What goes on outside the circle of grief seems shadowy, two-dimensional, not really there. Our bad habits come to the fore, we ruminate and obsess. To try to combat this I took to spending as much time as I could outside, walking, for hours. Relief came not so much with the miles accumulated, the exertion and tiredness that followed, but with the instants that punctuated the walks, the little surprises. A billow of rooks, a barn owl crossing the lane, sudden striations of light through leaves, the distant sound of a fox barking. A few months after Julia's diagnosis I crossed the river and saw swifts skid overhead for the first time that summer. Beneath was a line of swans, wings open, gliding downstream, a procession to welcome them back, one of the little miracles that we sometimes witness, like in the minutes after my father died, when a shower of soft rain tapped against the windows though there wasn't a cloud in the sky. I broke down in tears at the beauty and exquisite sadness of the world.

*

There's something about twilight that allows the past to slip into view more clearly, the way this day has slipped over the horizon with its tail still visible. The star Deneb shines above me, one of the brightest in the sky, a supergiant that would fill half the space between the sun and Earth. If it was as close to us as the other stars in the Cygnus constellation it would cast shadows like the moon. Deneb is from Arabic and means tail. It is so far away from us that we don't know if its light, which is touching my eyes, set out when the Roman Ptolemy recorded the forty-eight major constellations, or the Greek Hipparchus created the records that Ptolemy used as his source hundreds of years later. Perhaps this light was created further back when Eudoxus of Cnidus composed a poem about the constellations, the poem Hipparchus borrowed from, written almost two and a half millennia ago. As distances open up time slips backwards. We've been giving names to stars since our breath first made language, but we don't know where they are.

The Cygnus constellation is one of the most investigated areas of the sky. Astronomers have been pointing their telescopes at it for centuries and it has slowly revealed more and more of its secrets. There are several easily visible galaxies within it, also black holes and Earth-like planets that are orbiting their stars at a similar distance to ours. A luminous red nova is the term used for a collision of two stars, when the individual energy of both combines and a new, bigger star is created. The collision creates a distinct red colour with a fading wave of light haloing it. In 2017, a team of scientists at Calvin College, an American university, had been researching a binary star system within Cygnus called KIC 9832227. They discovered that the two stars were orbiting each other. Frequent eclipses occurred and the time between eclipses appeared to be getting shorter. After extensive calculations the team predicted that the stars would collide some time in 2022, creating a luminous red nova which would appear to us as a new star in the sky. This prediction went global. Many newspapers and magazines reported the discovery. Other scientists examined the data and agreed with the prediction, until one team went through the calculations carefully and realised that there had been a typographic error in the original data, throwing the calculations off completely. The birth of the new star has since been postponed, indefinitely. At an unknown point in the future, maybe years, maybe decades, maybe centuries from now, we will see, very faintly, on a particularly clear night, a tiny reddish dot above us that had not been there before. More accurately, the collision did or did not occur, and the light which is its proof has yet to reach us.

*

One of Caravaggio's early paintings depicts a young man bending over water to see his reflection. The youth's arms are spread and arced into the shape of the downbeat of a swan's wings. It is one of the master's first experiments with exaggerated light and shadow. The subject is not wholly visible, we see only the arc of his arms, shoulders and head, a bent knee coming out of a pure black background. This is a portrait of Narcissus, who has been staring at himself for many dawns and dusks. Perhaps this is the dead Narcissus whose ghost still peers into the black waters of the River Styx. Caravaggio's blending of parts of the figure into the background forces the viewer to create the youth's form the way we do when we see a shape in a star constellation, imagining a body from its luminous fragments. At first glance you'd think this is a dawn or dusk scene, the boy enveloped by a shadowed world, only half materialising in the little light that is present. But no twilight scene looks like this. I have watched swans at near dark, their whitest of white forms ghosted out against indigo-to-black water and sky, their edges blurred. They are like failing lanterns. Caravaggio's Narcissus is as luminous as the moon. The pallor of his skin and the fabric of his clothing beam out, bright enough to cast shadows. The viewer looks at the image through the artist's eyes as he gazes at a boy staring down at his reflection, which stares back. We're looking through four pairs of eyes, all of them seeing something different, and we're seeing all of those images at once. The last pair of eyes in the sequence, those of the reflected youth, are blind, made only from rebounding light. But the artist makes them see. His mission is to show the beauty of the things he makes, and how perfectly we are made. Everything else is excluded. The stream that must be eddying and snaking past the boy, the smooth stones and deep turf at its edge, the overhanging trees filled with watching birds, the coined patterns of the sky through leaves. All gone. Nature has been removed. Around the boy Caravaggio painted coat over coat of dark pigment, creating a black that refracts like deep water, a warm darkness that we can fold into. Stare at this scene long enough and we can convince ourselves that only we exist.

*

I'm taking a short cut to work through a small urban park where a boy sits on the grass staring at his mobile phone. He has just held it up to the sky and smiled into its camera. Now he corrects the image with the software, the hues, the sharpness and contrast, he smooths out his surroundings into a uniform, graduated background. In a second the horse chestnut tree behind him, which has just unfolded its first blazing leaves, melts away into a monotone background. In a minute he has a self-portrait he is happy with, an enhanced version of himself. He beams it out into electronic space, sharing it with the whole world, sharing it mostly with himself. He stands up, turns and walks away. He doesn't see me. He doesn't look up.

There is a line of thirty people gathered on a narrow path overlooking a deep cove on Skomer Island in west Pembrokeshire. They have taken a boat from the mainland, over a choppy sea, and climbed the steep cliff path to get here on a mid-June day of constant squalls. All around them are the scurrying shapes of puffins, little clowns, their huge beaks bright orange and yellow.

The birds wander in and out of their nesting burrows, or fly out over the cliff and down to the sea to hunt. Some return with beaks full of silver sand eels for their young. As they move around, almost at the spectators' feet, they purr and grumble. It is one of the great wildlife spectacles of the summer. But no one is watching. They all have their hands up in front of them, masking the space between themselves and the birds. What they see is mediated by a device, a camera or phone. It is as if their experience can only be real if it is recorded.

I'm sitting on a mudstone boulder resting on the glacier-cut sides of Hay Bluff, looking out over the Wye Valley far below and across a haze-free sky to the distant peaks of the Cambrian Mountains. A car has pulled up on the track below. A couple get out and lay a yoga mat on the ground. The woman arranges herself on the mat and strikes a pose, one leg raised high, a sort of vertical splits, one hand holding one foot. She tilts her head sideways, as if gazing at the mountain peak. Her partner is down on his knees in front of her, holding up his phone, taking shot after shot as she tries new positions. They stand up. The mat is rolled and put into the back of the car. The couple sit in the front seats. I watch them staring at the little rectangle of light, flicking between shots and choosing the best one. They press the share button. The car starts. They drive on to the next suitable background.

On the mountainside there is a thorn tree which has somehow managed to survive the ravages of upland winters in this bare, wind-scoured place. A female buzzard is perched, almost invisible, in its top branches. It has seen the couple in the car, but has taken almost no notice of them. They are not of this place. It is hungry. Over the preceding months it has reared two young. They have now fledged, but it is still providing food for them. For the past hour it has been resting, its yellow eyes flicking shut, sliding open to check on the sounds of cars on the pass and the wild ponies that occasionally approach to graze beneath the tree. Now its head turns quickly left and right as it scans the sky and takes in the wind. It opens its wings and dives out beyond the thorn tree, sliding on the cushion of air that rises up the steep slope. It rows out for a moment to gain height, then locks its wings. Already it is high above the valley floor. Though its wings and tail are motionless its head rotates from side to side, its eyes scanning the mountain, boring into the shadows beneath the gorse and bracken, searching for the slightest movement. It turns five, six wide circles then descends, crossing a plantation of pine trees down into the farmland below, following a steep lane with a high hedge on either side. It has seen movement in the grass. It fixes on it and folds its wings, then dives silently down to the lane where it thumps into a mound of earth and grips a mouse. Its hunger has made it disregard the two walkers who are coming up the lane. Immediately it is in flight again, a fury of wingbeats then a glide as it twists, spreads and flattens to pass between the rusted bars of a gate, then down a steeply sloping field to a fence post where it lands and feeds.

The buzzard is a point of pure attention, of awareness without self-awareness, its senses radiating out into the world to meet the senses of other creatures, the tiny mammals it feeds on, the other birds, insects and trees, the wild grasses and flowers that also radiate their awareness to make this place a vast network of attention.

*

There is a path from our house that goes a short distance into a wood thickly planted with pines and always dark, saturated with the blue light of dusk. On the floor beneath the trees nothing grows and each winter rainwater cuts deeper runnels into the ground, exposing layered fragments of mudstone. Once I came face to face with a badger here, in the very last light of a June day. Once a fox ran past me and my infant son, chased by a pack of hounds and another pack of men, each carrying a shotgun. We heard the guns go off a minute later and found the torn-up body by a stream. Once, wandering through the half-dark, trying to find the badger's set, I came across a buzzard's skull in a blanket of pine needles. Above me were the remains of a nest, a metre-wide tangle which had been abandoned. The skull must have been the remains of an almost fully fledged chick (three-quarters of buzzards don't survive their first year). It was pure white, translucent as porcelain, almost weightless. The hooked beak was dagger sharp, but what drew me in were the two huge voids where the buzzard's eyes had been. They still seemed to contain the bird's gaze. As I turned the skull in my hands I could feel its stare, fixing the needled ground and the feathered gaps between the pine trees. Everything surrounding me seemed to be sucked in by those blank sockets which were still

reading, reading, reading the terrain. I took it home and for many days afterwards it sat on a bookshelf facing out into the room where I write. Even with my back turned I could feel it watching. In the end I had to find a container for it, a little jewellery box that fitted the dimensions of the skull perfectly. I would occasionally open it, take out the jewel and turn it in my hands for a while, before putting it back, slightly spooked by the experience.

There is something accusatory in the stare of a buzzard. Those eyes, which can resolve details we will never witness, seem also to be telling us that something has gone wrong with our gaze, that we've trained our eyes almost exclusively on ourselves. As a result the multitudes of species and lifeways our planet has evolved are being driven to extinction.

Once, on a school holiday, the minibus I was travelling in ploughed into a stooping owl on the road. We kids inside only heard the thud as it collided. It happened so fast that the teacher who was driving didn't see what we had run into and we didn't know what had happened until we stopped at a service station and found the dead bird still attached to the radiator grill. I had never been so close to a wild owl. Its body was completely intact. I stroked its barred feathers, its black talons and beak. The creature was so light, so fragile, it felt as if it had no interior, that it wasn't real. I wanted to keep it, take it home, preserve the body somehow so I could examine the magical thing up close. But I had already had my turn and other kids wanted to see it. It was eventually passed to a boy who took out a penknife, cut off its foot to keep as a lucky charm and threw the rest of the corpse on to the road to watch it get crushed by passing cars. It is this utter lack of compassion for other species, this blindness, which has brought us to where we are, inhabitants of the landscapes of loss.

*

In a room with tiny windows letting in only a sepia pool of light, a man sits at a crude wooden lathe which he turns with one hand. In the other he holds a small blank of glass against a rotating mould which he coats with a paste containing different grades of sand. Slowly he grinds the glass into a shape, its uniformity and accuracy judged by eye. It is the act of a craftsman, like a potter or a silversmith, taking a material and transforming it slowly into something useful and beautiful. It takes many hours for the grinding and many more for the polishing to be complete. The room is pooled with shadow long before dark. Objects blend and fuse with their backgrounds. A rickety trestle table stands next to a wall. On it are dirty cloths, pots of grit and powder. On a stand at the edge of the table are rows of lenses, perfectly polished, concave and convex, little bowls and hemispheres. Some reflect their own interiors, others contain the whole of the room, ceiling, windows, doors, the craftsman bending to his work. The man now stands up from his stool carrying the newly made lens. He goes to the table and lifts another lens. He walks to the window, holds one lens up, then the other. For a second the two come into alignment and an image of a distant building suddenly magnifies.

In 1608, a lens grinder named Hans Lippershey invented the

telescope. Word spread among local lens makers, and then more widely. Two years later Galileo published 'Starry Messenger', in which he reported his observations of the moon, Jupiter and the Milky Way. Working with the glassmakers of Murano he created his own telescopes by grinding flat pieces of glass against an indented mould or a spherical object like a cannon ball. Initially an 8x magnification refraction telescope was created, then one of 20x magnification. With these tools he would prove the heliocentric nature of Earth. By 1616, the astronomer Niccolò Zucchi had invented the reflecting telescope, using curved mirrors. A few years later he discovered coloured belts on Jupiter and spots on Mars. By the mid seventeenth century, Isaac Newton had also created a reflecting telescope having invented his own technique for polishing mirrors.

The making of lenses was central to the development of the Enlightenment. The philosopher Spinoza spent decades of his life working on his theory of an infinitely creative and objective universe not subject to the control of an anthropomorphic god, while making a living as a lens grinder. His lenses were well known for their accuracy and high degree of finish. In his writing Spinoza didn't refer to his profession, but crafting objects to enhance the human gaze must have been a source for his clear-sighted metaphysics.

Spinoza lived only a few miles away from Antonie van Leeuwenhoek, who, perhaps inspired by the philosopher, quietly, and with a refusal to participate with the revered universities and societies of his day, refined his own process of manufacturing tiny lenses in an attempt to create a device which would allow him to see the magnified details of natural objects. The dissected silk-creating organs of spiders were fixed to a needle which could be moved by the turning of screws, nearer to and further from the lens. It was the first microscope. Through some of the almost five hundred that he made in his lifetime Leeuwenhoek was the first human to see bacteria and protozoa.

Lenses and mirrors developed quickly in accuracy and magnification and the human gaze penetrated deeper into the microcosms and macrocosms of the universe. We mounted telescopes on towers, then created them the size of buildings and built them on the tops of extinct volcanoes. We put them into rockets and sent them out of Earth's atmosphere. We built them to detect radio waves instead of light so that we could study stars in the daytime. Galaxies appeared, spiral nebulae, black holes. On the microcosmic scale we discovered the cellular basis of life. Our light microscopes evolved to magnify an image up to two thousand times before we harnessed accelerated electrons, increasing magnification to ten million times.

We've peered into the vast machinery of life, but at the same time our surroundings have retreated. The beings we share space with, the creatures that fly over us, dig beneath us, speak to us in their own languages, have grown distant. They have become obstacles on our fantastic journey.

*

There is a camera pointed through an open window facing the sea. We are peering through its lens at a stone harbour, at cliffs and a beach. They are barely visible against the rain which is coming down hard and almost horizontal. We are not sure if it is dawn or dusk. Yachts are swaying and lurching, ramming each other. The harbour will not protect them against this storm. Waves batter the walls, overtopping them, sending spray a hundred feet high, flying inland, mixing with the rain which has already choked every gutter, every drain. The ocean surface is smashed up, tones of lead mixing with foam-white scrawls. A giant wave lunges in and rolls right over the harbour wall, landing on the leaking roofs. Tiles lift and slide. Seawater rushes into houses. The next wave lifts two boats and throws them on to the street.

There is a line of palm trees on the seafront. They are bent away from the wind, their fronds shredding. Through the camera they look like underwater weeds attached to the seabed. Around them tin cans, bottles, newspapers, old shoes, washed-up waste from fishing boats scurry across the ground like vermin. There are birds here, a flock of white gulls using the eddies under the cliffs to rush up and out and down, like more blown debris. Through the whoosh and howl of the microphone we can just hear their cries. They are victims of the storm and we are not, though we created it. We are watching this scene on a computer screen or television, part of a newsreel, or a video embedded in a web page. We stare for a little while and then something else takes our attention. The storm is a long way away, on the other side of the world. Here the sun has gone down, the light has almost drained from the sky. Not a breath of wind. Stars begin to appear.

*

Perhaps they were blown off course in a storm, or their internal navigation went astray, or they were forced to move into new territory. Three juvenile tundra swans who had spent the summer in Alaska headed south into the Pacific Ocean, rather than inland towards the temperate regions of Canada and the USA, where they would normally spend the winter. Swans are not birds we associate with pelagic travel, but this trio managed to fly three thousand miles across the Pacific to Hawaii. They were discovered feeding in the Kaua'i Lagoons area, close to the island's airport, in October 2003. Two days later one of the birds was captured and the other two shot by employees of the US Department of Agriculture who considered them to be a risk to aircraft. According to the ornithological records for Hawaii it seems that swans make this journey approximately twice each decade, though they have never been allowed to breed on the islands.

The Hawaiian Islands are located over a volcanic hotspot on the Pacific plate. Most volcanic activity occurs on the edges of tectonic plates, where one is pulling away from, sliding against or subsuming another. But this hotspot sits in the middle of the plate. Below is a mantle plume, a superheated subterranean zone which melts rock and forms areas of magma which push up through minor faults. Volcanoes appear beneath the surface of the ocean and slowly rise, layer on layer, until they form island masses. As they slowly grow, the tectonic plate inches away from them, moving the hotspot away. As a result of this process a chain of islands has formed which tracks in the north-west direction of the plate. The volcanoes go from being vigorously active, to occasionally active, to dormant and eventually extinct. The islands Ni'ihau and Kaua'i formed between 5.6 and 3.8 mya (million years ago); neighbouring O'ahu between 3.4 and 2.2 mya; Moloka'i, 1.8 and 1.3 mya; Maui, 1.3 and 0.8 mya. Hawai'i began forming less than 0.7 mya and is still growing. Nearby, to the south-east, a new island, Lō'ihi, is coming up from the surface of the ocean. Given their location in the middle of Earth's fiercest ocean the islands erode rapidly as they age. Their mountain peaks crumble away. In a few million years, Ni'ihau and Kaua'i will sink back beneath the water and disappear. The once glaciated Mauna Kea, the world's tallest mountain if measured from its base on the ocean floor, will be worn down to a submerged stump. The profile of the island chain is a jagged version of the arc of the sun, a geological dawn, noon and dusk.

There is an ancient tree, a tree that will never have a name. It is rooted in dark soil on a sun-facing slope in a land that will become known as China. It has silver-blue bark and pedunculate leaves the shape of Zulu shields. The tree is tall and lean, and it bends like a bow in the wind. Hanging beneath its upper branches are clusters of tiny seed pods which are just beginning to break open. The pods are a blue-bronze hue that, once the tree is extinct, will never be seen on Earth again. Today the wind is coming from the mountains to the west, scouring the hillside in twisting squalls. The trunk leans and bends, the branches gesticulate. Each time it reaches out towards the sea it peppers millions of seeds into the air. Some land in fertile soil metres or kilometres away and will become next year's saplings, part of a forest that stretches to the Himalayan mountains. Others are blown into the sky to swirl for months up there, caught in subtropical thermals, heading out on an air current that flows all the way to the Arctic. They will be carried north and east. Some will then track south again, caught in a gyre a thousand miles wide. They will skim the edge of the North American continent and then travel to the centre of the Pacific. Most will fall uselessly into the ocean where they will be churned down into the depths. A few will return to the land they came from. A tiny amount of seeds, only a handful, will blow over a chain of volcanic islands to land in rich black soils and germinate. These trees will speciate rapidly. Eventually one of their descendants will become a Koa tree, the most common of endemic Hawaiian trees. This miraculous process, where a distant plant species appears for the first time on the islands, happens once every ninety thousand years.

The ecology of the Hawaiian Islands is unique and complex. Species have evolved here in isolation from their continental originators and have followed widely divergent paths of evolution due to the complexity of the volcanic landscape, which comprises distinct coastal, subtropical and alpine forest, and high-altitude desert zones. A recent study of the fossil record of the islands, combined with genetic sequencing, investigated an endemic tribe of birds known as honeycreepers. It was found that all had evolved from a single ancestor of the Asiatic rosefinch. Rosefinches are known to leave their traditional territories in large flocks to look for new breeding grounds. One flock must have made it from the eastern rim of Asia, across the Pacific to Hawaii. They adapted to ecological niches as the islands transformed, the birds evolving rapidly into almost sixty separate species. Their common traits were their size, bright colours and canary-like songs, but their adaptations were very different. Some of the birds had the beaks of parrots, others of warblers. Some had thin, straight beaks, others were profoundly down-curving. Some fed on nectar, others ate fruit, or snails, or seeds. In a rapidly transforming environment, where islands appeared, expanded, forested and deforested, where ice caps formed and melted creating wet environments, these birds responded with ever-changing survival adaptations. Over time they filled available niches, travelled to colonise new islands, then backfilled old territories when volcanic activity destroyed their existing ranges. Many honeycreeper species are now extinct and some of the remaining species are critically endangered. The arrival of humans on the islands has accelerated these extinctions, but the slow dwindling of the species, like the shrinking of the older islands in the chain, was long established.

It was originally believed that the islands had been inhabited by humans since around 300 CE, but a recent carbon-dating study showed that Polynesian sailors arrived less than eight hundred years ago. In the short amount of time since, the ecology of the islands has changed hugely. The Polynesians brought with them the plants that they needed to survive: coconut, sweet potato, banana, taro, sugar cane. Later waves of settlers brought pineapple, mango, papaya and passion fruit as well as orchid, ginger, jasmine and hibiscus. These plants rapidly overtook the endemic species. When Westerners began to colonise the islands, large amounts of cattle were imported. Now Hawai'i is home to one of the biggest cattle ranches in the USA. It is estimated that after our arrival one plant species went extinct every nine months. Of the 50,000 endemic plants on the islands only 2,500 remain and of these 30 per cent are endangered. The Hawaiian archipelago is Earth in miniature, demonstrating the complexities and creative randomness of speciation. The dawn of life on the island was followed by ever-greater enrichment. The gradual weaving and enmeshing of life filled the evolving landscape until it peaked and then began to slowly decline. A biological dusk arrived and, with the arrival of humans, it accelerated.

In 2020, the scientist Dr Andrea Ghez was awarded the Nobel Prize in physics for a quarter of a century's work studying black holes. Ghez and her team proved conclusively that there is a giant black hole at the centre of the Milky Way. Her work has been conducted almost exclusively at the Keck Observatory, one of the world's most powerful telescopes, located near the summit of Mauna Kea on Hawai'i. Its two mirrors weigh more than three hundred tons each and are made of honeycomb structures ten metres in diameter. Ghez's work observes the stars closest to the centre of our galaxy, recording how they orbit the seemingly empty space that they surround.

Mauna Kea is the best place on Earth to view the universe due to its four thousand-metre altitude, low latitude and the clarity of the surrounding atmosphere given the lack of light pollution and its position above the humid zone. A total of thirteen observatories have been built near its summit in a fifty-year period on a designated science reserve of several thousand acres. The early telescopes have become obsolete and the Keck Observatory itself is about to be superseded by a telescope three times its size.

Since their inception, the Hawai'ian telescopes have regularly been pointed at the Cygnus constellation. An area of the constellation which has been studied in great detail is known as Cygnus-X, a region of the Milky Way which has been birthing new stars in the most spectacular way. Infrared images of the region resemble a submarine environment filled with phosphorescent corals and swirling clouds of plankton. There are scattered stars of every colour and grade of luminosity. Red and blue gas clouds composed of millions of threads, each light years in length, resemble the churned surface of the ocean. These clouds are formed by solar winds generated by newly born stars. They could be cirrus clouds striated with red light at sunset, shredded by high-altitude winds. In the centre of one image of Cygnus-X is a gas cloud, elongated and curving, attached to a wider body which spreads across the frame. Out of this cloud, new suns will form and travel across the galaxy, a process which will take hundreds of millions of years. But in this instant it resembles the long neck and wide wings of a swan.

*

We Westerners spent a lot of our history thinking that the sun revolved around us. Then we learned it was we who are the travellers, and later that there are more suns, more worlds than it is possible to count or imagine. We know now that even the cratered satellite that orbits our planet contains enough water to harbour life. There are at least a hundred billion stars in the Milky Way and a similar number in every one of the ten billion observable galaxies in the universe. Is the human imagination, that mysterious entity which parallels so closely the endless creativity of nature, able to conjure images of life we will never witness? Let's think of birds. It is difficult to imagine an avian form which our own planet's myriad evolutionary paths have not already created. What else could there be out there that is more miraculous than a sunbird, a snowy owl, a hyacinth macaw? Even when I look at the varieties within a single species I struggle to imagine variants that have not already been created. Look at the pigeon for instance, which, where I live, is the most ordinary of birds. Worldwide, there are almost three hundred species of pigeon, each with its unique colours and iridescences. There is the pink pigeon of Mauritius with its pale rose head and breast. And the Japanese wood pigeon with its sooty wings, its green and purple neck. The streamlined, plover-like, Namaqua dove of sub-Saharan Africa. Australia is home to the spinifex pigeon with its lapwing crest, and the common bronzewing, which has secondary feathers splashed with sun-bright orange. The wompoo fruit dove of the west coast has a red and yellow beak, purple and yellow undersides. There are pigeons and doves with every colour combination you can think of. They have plumes and crests, elongated tails and topknots, feathered manes and bleeding hearts. Perhaps the most spectacular of all is the Victoria crowned pigeon with its amazing fanned crest, more detailed and delicate than the finest Koniaków lace. These are just a few species of one family, within a single order of birds. The endless shapes and sizes, colouration, calls and songs of other orders are myriad: gulls, shrikes and mockingbirds; wagtails, owls and swallows; cranes, divers and frigatebirds; flycatchers, orioles and bustards.

I'm doing my best to imagine a species of bird on a planet like ours, but utterly different, thousands of light years away. I imagine this planet spins on a more oblique axis to its sun so that twilight in its northerly and southerly regions lasts for days. Here evolution has favoured creatures which can create their own light. Its oceans glow, lit by clouds of algae. In its strange forests trees have evolved needles which shine like Christmas decorations. And in its skies are great birds blocking out the pointillist patterns of the surrounding galaxies. The birds have long necks and wide wings. They are covered with phosphorescent feathers, standing out against the sky, like luminous swans or comets.

*

There is a camera mounted on a spacecraft which has travelled almost four billion miles to the edge of the solar system and is about to enter interstellar space. Its mission is almost over. It has sent startling images back to us of seven undiscovered moons, new rings on Saturn and Jupiter, active volcanoes on Io spewing clouds of sulphur into space. Now the scientists have been persuaded to use it one last time before it is powered down. The camera takes three frames at different exposures, each with a different coloured filter. When combined, a scene appears of empty space fanned with diagonal rays of light. In the centre-right of the frame is a tiny blemish, a single bad pixel among 640,000 others. It is the faintest glow of an ember about to go dark, an indeterminate, shapeless thing. This image of Earth's pale blue dot has become famous.

The spacecraft, *Voyager 1*, is still travelling through the galaxy, though it is now ten billion miles further away than when it took its last image. It is still sending information back to us, raw data from its instruments which, powered with only a trickle of energy, function nevertheless. Its cameras haven't been used for thirty years. The craft is travelling at fifty times the speed of sound through a starlit void. Barring a collision with space debris or being drawn into orbit by another star, it will continue on its journey indefinitely. Though its instrumentation will go dead in 2025 it could still be travelling when humans have become extinct, when Earth has transformed into a planet inhabited by life forms we would not recognise. It may become the last existing human creation, still extant long after the sun has burned through its fuel and become a red giant, consuming Mercury, Venus and Earth. In the meantime it hurtles blind through an emptiness we, though having access to the data, can never comprehend.

On a wall at NASA's Theodore von Kármán Auditorium is a twenty-feet-wide mosaic of the famous image. When people pass it they reach up to touch the blue dot. It's become such a habit that the tiny point wears through occasionally and the panel has to be replaced every few years. We're proud that even the vast planet that evolved us over billions of years from the tiniest microbial organism can now appear to us like that organism, featureless and insignificant. Our gaze is so far from where we are. We reach out to touch the blue dot, our fingers smothering it and everything it is host to.

*

Cygnus has flown a few degrees north. There are bands of cloud moving in from the east, smothering some of the constellations that have now become visible. I'm once again scanning the sky with my binoculars, using the roof of the car to steady my hands so I can see even the faintest stars. The corona of daylight is fading now, but it is still just visible. Dogs are barking on a nearby farm and something wild has just made a noise I've never heard before, part shriek, part howl. An involuntary shiver goes through me and the stars blur. My eyes are watering from staring for so long. I'm irritated by my lack of attention; the urge to jump into the car and start for home has almost got the better of me several times in the past hour. I was expecting the comet to be luminous, something sparkling on the horizon like a firework. I use the compass again, repositioning myself as a finger of cloud moves closer to where the comet should be. And then Neowise appears. It is higher than I had thought. Now I can see its twin tails, one long and curved, made from the dust it constantly emits as it slowly dissipates into space. The other gas tail, formed by the solar wind, is shorter and straight, with a hint of blue. I continue to stare through the binoculars, nervous to blink in case it disappears. It's the first time in my life that I've witnessed a comet. It is the faintest of phenomena, two-dimensional, a point and the slip of a pen. Though it was only discovered a few months ago we already know that it is a long-period comet with an eccentric orbit taking almost seven thousand years to complete. The last time it entered our sky we may have thought it was a god. The next time we may again think it is a god, or we may not be here. Tomorrow the image of it will be seen by hundreds of millions of eyes, not looking up at the night sky, but staring into screens. It will be shared, reshared. And quickly forgotten.

LIGHT UNDER LEAVES

John opens his back door and walks into the courtyard between his house and barn. Swallows are perched on the wire strung between the two buildings. It is late summer and soon they will be gone from the shed where they have been nesting for all the fifty years he's lived here. He goes to the gate and checks the yard where two horses stand with their heads draped and their tails flicking, miserable from the constant attacks of biting flies. He checks the water trough and pats each horse, then walks into the field and follows a fence which he's been meaning to repair all summer. At the bottom of the field is another gate, rusted and bent, held closed with a loop of twine. He opens it and walks out on to wilder ground. The cropped grass is replaced by tangles of brambles, sedge spikes and bracken grown head high. He follows the narrow path the feet of his family and the hooves of his horses have created over the years towards an oak tree which fans out and dominates the foreground, obscuring the view across the wide valley to the mountain peaks beyond. John remembers how it used to look from this spot where he now pauses. There were no obstacles between the long wall of the mountains and his fields when he came here. Now the place has come back to life, transforming into a wood of oak, birch, ash and rowan. It seems to have grown so slowly, and yet it's strange how high and tangled it's become within the lifetimes of his children. He walks into the tunnel between the trees. There are new species arriving all the time. A crab apple has grown on the edge of the path and now it is heavy with hard fruit. Beneath it there are still the remains of last year's crop, forming a pale green circle below the tree. A jay scatters in front of him, cackling as it disappears into the thick of an ash. There is a blackbird singing overhead, watched by the cloak and dagger form of a buzzard perched on the highest branches of a tree he climbed once, years ago, when it was only half as high. He comes to a stand of young rowans, spindly, tall and so covered with berries the air is stippled red. The fieldfares will arrive soon, a swarm of them that will clear the berries quickly. At his feet are toadstools even redder than the berries, each one covered with white spots, most of them with little crescents bitten out of them by the teeth of mice. The floor of the wood is full of them. Every year more colour. The bluebells this spring were thicker than previous years and had started to invade the horse pasture. There were dog roses, wood violets, anemones and flowers he didn't know the names of. There was a big storm, earlier in the year. The wind blew down a fork-trunked oak in the middle of the wood. The tree split at the cleft and fell. John heard it from his house, even as the storm raged, and felt the ripple through the ground as it landed. There is a space in the canopy now, a wide oval where the tree used to be. It feels strange to him to stand at this opening to the glare of the white sky. It's better in the shadows beneath the leaves. Under the trees it feels, somehow, as if there's a conversation going on, just audible, but one he's part of.

*

Hazel trees line the stream on one side, overhanging the falls where I've been waiting all day, wet and freezing. My fingers are seized, my camera hanging heavily from my neck. If a salmon appeared now I wouldn't be able to press the shutter release. I should be home, in front of the wood burner, watching its orange light spread into the room. But something else is keeping me here. I haven't seen a salmon in years. To spot them fleetingly, one or two immature fish struggling upstream, when there should be thousands, tens of thousands, saddens me. Years ago, on another continent, I crossed a bridge over a stream like this and saw a big school of them, crowded together, swaying to hold against the current, so many they were like the scales of a single fish.

There's something about places like this, where the trees hang over fast-moving water. They hold on to their absences somehow, particularly at dusk. I'm only metres from the road. There are electricity and telephone wires strung between high poles. In the stream is the detritus of our lives only just beginning its long decomposition: plastic drink bottles, feed buckets, haylage wrappers, old shoes, barbed wire. From a low branch on an oak hangs a frayed nylon rope tied to it years ago, long enough for the bark to have bulged either side of the spool and knot. It will still be there a century from now. Among the pebbles on the stream bed are pieces of glass and pottery, their edges ground smooth. On the other side of the water the slices and subdivisions of land are clear, lines of grown-out hedges, reinforced with post and wire all the way up the slope to the hard edge of a fir plantation. These details are receding with the twilight. As shadow closes around me the memory of the place grows, pushing out of the ground like saplings. There was a forest here once, before the Brythonic language shaped itself on the tongues of the Celts, before the Romans built roads and forts nearby, before Christian monks came to build hermitages and places of worship. Juniper, alder, pine, birch, willow, hazel, oak, holly, ash, rowan, blackthorn. These species colonised the ground in waves, forming a temperate rainforest which teemed with insects, birds and mammals. In autumn the salmon migration would have been at its peak, fish running from the Severn Sea, up the rivers Usk, Taff, Ely, Rhonda, Thaw, Wye, before those places had names. The fish climbed into the uplands via ladders of water. Bears would be waiting for them, gripping rocky edges, leaning down into white water to catch a leaping fish in their jaws.

The nourishment of a coastal rainforest is at its peak when the salmon return. Studies in British Columbia have found particulate traces of salmon in trees miles away from the nearest watercourse. The salmon feed the forest via the creatures that predate them. The roots of the word nourish go back through Old English *norishen*, to drink or feed, through Latin *nutrire*, to nurse, suckle or let flow, and further back to the Proto-Indo-European word *(s)nau*, which meant to swim. Salmon were still nourishing this place less than a century ago. Many great fish were caught on the River Wye in the decades between the two world wars. The largest fish found in the area weighed approximately eighty pounds. The last fish recorded at above fifty pounds was caught three years before I was born. The only salmon left on Earth of a comparable size are Pacific Chinook salmon in the remote rivers of Alaska.

It's not difficult to imagine, particularly now the light is low, the fish that ran up this stream, how the now-vanished forest transformed to meet them, sending out all of its inhabitants to gather the nutrients it needed to feed the trees. If we were to retreat for a while and find ways to feed ourselves that don't demand so much of the wild, the salmon-nourished forest would regrow here.

Our memory of a place graduates like the light. It's not too hard for me to recall the reflecting silver of the salmon, but there are other creatures which have slipped back into the deeper shadows. This was part of the great border forest, home to the last wolves in England and Wales. There are few stories of them, though they were still here when some of the old oaks which stand in the fields were saplings. It's in the nature of forests to hold on to their denizens, to fold them into the leaf shade, hiding them until they're ready to be discovered. But the wolf didn't disappear into the forest, the forest disappeared with the wolf, cut back to let the light in, to make these bare fields which are now the dominant feature of one of the least biodiverse countries on Earth. There is no place for the wolf here, and no place for the forest. They were bleached out by the glare. In this landscape, at twilight, the emptiness is exposed.

*

Douglas fir, amabilis fir, western hemlock, Sitka spruce, red cedar. There is a place I dream of frequently, a place with the magical name of Great Bear Rainforest. It is one of the last areas of unspoiled temperate forest on Earth, a place where wild land meets wild ocean in the Canadian Pacific Northwest. Though it is ten thousand miles from here it feels almost familiar, being a place of fast-running rivers and steep valleys, of mists and feathered light. It could almost be home, the way home once was. There are packs of wolves in the forest that have never encountered a human being. The steep fjords and coastal estuaries are inhabited by sea otters, orcas and humpback whales. I dream of it while I sit on a high hill, scraped bare of trees. It's a source of wonder to me knowing that there is somewhere out there where the ancient forest canopy still creates a green twilight at noon.

There is a photograph of the Great Bear Rainforest I look at often. It shows a steep valley fringed with snow-capped mountains. Through the middle of it runs a blue river. A blanket of trees reaches high up the slopes on either side. There is no sign of a road or track. But there are ancient tracks beneath the canopy that humans have used for hundreds of generations. They meander and wind like the streams they follow, passing beneath ancient trees, some fifteen hundred years old. I like to imagine what the light is like beneath those ancient trees, the sounds they make, the animal species that intertwine with them. I often read lists of them the way I used to slowly turn the pages of my animal encyclopedia when I was a boy, reading out the names slowly: long-toed salamander, coastal tailed frog, northern flying squirrel, bushy-tailed woodrat, hoary marmot, American pika. There are hundreds of bird species as exotic to me as toucans and turacos: evening grosbeaks, white-winged crossbills, grey-crowned rosy-finches, dark-eyed juncos, ruby-crowned kinglets, red-eyed vireos, eastern kingbirds. My imagination can swim inside these names. The bird I would love to see most, perched on a wire above my house, is the violet-green swallow, the cousin of the common swallow. They spend their summers glinting in the twilight of the ancient forest, their markings bathed in the graduated colours of a sky after the sun has dipped below the horizon, the strange blue-greens, yellow-bronzes and pink-purples that mix, transform and separate continually. Each bird has a breastplate as pale as the rising moon.

The best place I know to watch swallows is the warehouse of a local builder's merchant. The birds flit in and out of the space constantly from late April until September, circling the forklift trucks and circular saws, perching on cross beams and nesting beneath the metal roof. Others spend their summers in a friend's barn above queues of dead tractors, piles of scrap metal, old caravans and horse boxes. They are agile birds, able to dive and wheel in tight spaces, skills evolved in the ancient forests where they nested in tree holes and hawked for insects between the branches. The tightest space I've ever seen them in is the toilet block at Martin's Haven, where people catch the boat to Skomer Island. Above the cubicles and inside the doorways are a row of mud nests, which, during the summer, are filled with several broods, the young swallows gaping wildly while the parent birds swoop in, feed them and dive out again only centimetres above people's heads. A swallow's flight is always complex, a slalom run low over the grass, or a series of feints, dives and double-backs. They negotiate an invisible obstacle course. It's as if they know where the trees should be.

*

Prickly featherwort, whipwort, straggling pouchwort, barnacle lichen. The call of Canada geese above the trees. A single bird flies into view, panic-stricken, hurtling towards the almost vertical cliff on the other side of the reservoir. Perhaps it has encountered one of the peregrine falcons that stalk the valley. I follow it with my binoculars and watch it turn at the last minute, brushing the side of the rocks before climbing and going over the summit. High above it two buzzards are circling on a thermal. It is mating season, a pair of ravens in the pine trees sending broken love notes to each other, hidden from view. Smaller birds I can't identify flick into view then disappear into the shadows of the wood. The high path follows the edge of the water, with a cliff on one side. I'm looking at the colours of the stones, at the lichens and bryophytes which grow everywhere on the rocks and trees. Their fecundity and diversity identify this valley as one of the last remnants of Atlantic rainforest in Wales.

Look at a map of Earth's temperate rainforests and you will see what a tiny proportion of the globe they occupy, thin strips of coastal land in the cool and wet areas of continents and islands, Western Canada, New Zealand, Japan, Patagonia. Wales, the Scottish Highlands and Ireland are prime locations in Europe. The forest hasn't existed intact in Wales for five millennia, and yet there are some places, tiny islands, which still hang on. Coed Cwm Elan is one of four acknowledged Celtic rainforest areas in Wales, though even here there are only fragments which match the definition. On either side of the reservoir there are oak woods reaching up the valley walls. From where I'm standing, looking across the water, they resemble the puddled shapes of lichens. They border faces of rock, heather and bilberry moors, pasture and pine plantations. The zones are hard-edged, the greys of oaks, blues of stone, greens of pasture, almost blacks of firs.

I'm trying to concentrate on the close-up details of the lichens, which seem almost infinite in tone and shape. The closer I get to them the more I'm drawn in. On one face of stone I count twenty different varieties, six on a single tree bole standing next to it, together with three bryophytes, which I believe are featherworts. I have no expertise in this area and I'm finding it hard to differentiate between multiple species and the varieties within a single species, they're so tangled and multifarious. I spot one I can identify, the pearl-white sea shape of the barnacle lichen. I climb a little slope of scree and peer at a rectangular shelf of stone, reaching out to run a finger along the surface, the burst bubble texture, hard as glaze. The lichen seems impregnable, yet they are fragile organisms, growing sparsely, in ancient woodlands with the cleanest air, spreading as little as half a millimetre each year.

I enter into an area of oaks beyond the rocks and climb a steep, stony path between cushions of bilberry. The trees are not old, it is perhaps less than a century since they seeded, but they have been colonised by hundreds of species of lichen and bryophyte. Every trunk, branch and twig is covered. In places they look as if they've grown fur, or been spattered with pigment from an artist's brush: gold, copper, pearl, sulphur, lime, lemon. I pick up a fallen branch, feather-light with rot. On its underside, where it has been lying on the ground, it has been picked clean and looks like driftwood. But on top is a forest of miniature trees, an overstorey of feathery moss, a ground of lichens. An expert could probably identify thirty species here. The branch has become an ecosystem, part of a web of ecosystems within an island of trees.

It takes me five minutes to come to the edge of the wood and I'm out on to an open heath, the path leading up to a summit four hundred metres above me. From the top you can see the reservoir, the water stretching out like a melt of lead, revealing the shape of the valley. Away to the north is the ruler edge of the lower dam, a little river beyond. To the south is the upper dam, a black, slick rampart. From time to time they move water from the upper to the lower reservoir. Gates open and water bursts out, cataclysmic in scale, a thousand water canons turned to maximum. It channels through the lower levels of the woods, kicking up spray which thins, mists and spreads in the understorey. The green air beneath the canopy refracts, bending light around the miniature forests which grow on every twig making tiny rainbows and sunsets, landscapes of life miniaturised.

*

Birch trees. I am sitting on the ground in John's wood, watching and listening. The canopy that birches create is thin, a spatter of green blown against the sky. But there is a graduated light beneath them, here at ground level. A layer of bracken surrounds the roots of the trees, different than the bracken that grows outside of the tree shade. There the fronds are head height, growing thick and tangled, fighting for light. Beneath the canopy they only grow to knee height and they're spread evenly, almost politely, like miniature trees in a toy park. It is windless in the wood but the fronds are moving to a subterranean tremor, a pulse. Each responds differently, depending on the complexities of its shape and the pocket of air which it occupies. I could try to describe this phenomena, but I would fail. All I know is that this place of dappled twilight, away from the glare, is somewhere I can find peace.

It is the hottest day of summer so far, thirty degrees in the shade, too hot for these wet hills. But under the canopy it is cool, tranquil. Across the world weather systems are intensifying. In the west of Canada, close to the Great Bear Rainforest, the trees are cooking beneath atmospheric domes trapping warm air and heating it to extreme temperatures. Parts of Europe are caught inside another weather system which is creating slow-moving storm fronts holding huge amounts of moisture, releasing it in torrential downpours which are tearing rivers apart and drowning whole valleys. Villages have been smashed by the flood waters, houses washed away. The oscillations of the weather swing ever more violently.

Though it is high summer I'm inhabiting a self-created half-light. A wave of mental illness has swept over me. The climate crisis is one factor but three years of continual family crises, of losses and near losses, sickness, partial recoveries and relapses have been the main cause. At the moment I can't see a way through the anxiety. Depression is sometimes described as an atmosphere. A cloud or a mist. But it's bigger than that. It contains climates, weathers. It can be tropical or temporal. You can burn or freeze, be soaked to the skin, blown sideways. When I'm depressed I can sometimes become so blind to other people's suffering that I shrug at the worst tragedies. At other times I break down at the slightest thing, passing a torn curtain in a window, an empty playground, an abandoned toy. Weeks go by when I'm swallowed whole, when the only way out, it seems, is shutdown. I could sleep for days. I could drink for weeks. I do neither because there's work to do.

In the last years there have been a few local suicides, middle-aged men like me who have been consumed by their mental illness. Two of them hung themselves in the woods. Though I've never considered suicide myself I've often wondered if one of the big dives that I experience will one day plunge me too low and lead me towards it. It's unlikely, the world is too beautiful and I want to be here for as long as possible. It would certainly not happen in a wood.

The birches are starting to sway a little, a breeze getting up, a storm coming. The wood is on the move, the ten thousand things trembling with life. The deadness inside me falls away for an instant as I watch and listen. If I could stay entranced like this for an hour or a day, the dark and dreamless sleep of depression might slope away, like a predator given the slip.

Cancer cells move in the body like particles in sap, following the tributaries of the blood vessels and the lymph system. The diagnosis for Julia when a mammogram located a one-centimetre lesion in her left breast. Tests followed to confirm this and to identify the form of cancer, which was stage 1. Though it had been caught early, the cancer cells were no longer contained within the tumour and could possibly have spread into the lymph system. The tumour was also oestrogen positive, which meant that an ongoing treatment for pre-cancerous cells in her womb, which boosted oestrogen levels, had to be curtailed and post-operative treatment for both conditions would be complicated. Treatment for one could exacerbate the other. The operation to remove the tumour was straightforward and Julia recovered from it quickly. Radiotherapy followed, with days of driving to and from the hospital for a treatment which was painless initially but built up to create many painful side effects.

While we waited to be called into the therapy room we sat in a large area with many other cancer patients. Some were clearly very sick. No one spoke to each other, except for faint, whispered and brief conversations between patients and the friends or family members who accompanied them. A large television hovered above everyone's heads, showing vacuous game shows, the news and weather. The volume was turned down to an inaudible level. But we all seemed to be drawn to it, a distraction from the realities of the disease which, I'm sure we all thought, not everyone in the room would survive. The fear that it might be themselves or their loved one was present in every eye. At the door was a metal bell. When any patient completed their treatment they rang the bell on the way out of the building. As they did, all the doctors, nurses and staff clapped cheerfully. When it was Julia's turn she rang it softly, a little embarrassed to draw attention to herself. Then we walked away from the building as fast as we could.

But cancer doesn't end with the ring of a bell. The disease has half-lives, much like radioactive material, or declining trees. Recovery is slow and doesn't feel like recovery for a long time. Often there are complications, other conditions are triggered, more tests required and long waits for results. For me this was the worst part of the process, my imagination branching out in every direction at the possibilities, most of them awful. Those mental processes can only lead you one way, down into the dark.

*

I've been to forests filled with hyraxes, vipers, monkeys and elephants. But the forest of my imagination is the one that is hiding beneath my feet, in these hills, waiting to regrow. The trees are garlanded with sea-green mosses and bracketed with fungi. Their branches are filled with blackbirds, jays and wrens. There are dormice nesting in hollows, fallow deer invisible beneath boughs, streams edged with forked roots sheltering the holts of otters. There are foxes and badgers and, somewhere just out of sight, wild cats, wolves, bears. Storms roll over it, the canopy slides and rocks. It is calm.

Desert dwellers imagine in drifts. They see mirages shifting on undulating horizons, huge stones floating just above the ground. Their colours are sand silver, sand red, sky blue. City dwellers imagine the shapes behind glass. They see around corners, through doors and walls. They picture what they hear in conversations which drift past them as they walk down a crowded street. But in this place, where the forest used to be, people imagine in tendrils and forks, down into the ground and up into the air. Our colours are translucent, stained glass, ink on paper. Our horizons are obscured. The windows of our imaginations are not straight-sided, rectangular or uniform. They shift in the wind and are edged with leaves.

There is a place by the river where my boys and I used to walk at dusk, along a track that cut into a steep-sided slope overgrown with high, spindly trees. Webs of ivy grew between the trees and brambles cosseted the understorey. We had to stick to the path because the wood was almost impenetrable. The river ran invisible but audible below. Night descended here sooner than anywhere else in the valley. There was a badgers' set in the wood and we often sat nearby waiting for them to appear, which they never did, it being too difficult for two little boys to remain quiet for long enough. On the way home we kept our torches off and even the owls couldn't see us through the tight weave of the leaves. They called to each other from branches only a few feet above, so loud we could almost hear them inhale. When one did finally spook away from us we could feel the air on its wings rush across our faces. I don't think I ever saw my boys as enchanted, so simultaneously engaged by their senses and imaginations, which flowed out, making shapes in the owled spaces of the twilit wood.

*

Ginkgo, camphor, Chinese cedar, katsura, dawn redwood. In the markets of the Jingdezhen area of northern China it is common for sellers to transport the remains of trees from nearby forests to sell as household features and ornaments. Fallen branches, sawn-off trunks and twisted roots of every shape and size are exhibited and purchased. The artist Ai Weiwei began buying some of these objects after a visit to the area and stored them in the grounds of his studio for years until, in 2009, he began to use them to create fabricated sculptures. He joined together several species in each piece, attaching them using crude joints fixed with metal bolts. The finished sculptures have been exhibited together as collections, forests in miniature, in the great galleries and city spaces of the world. They are works of power, Frankensteinian facsimiles of their original forms, barkless, bleached, cut and spliced. There is a sense of suffering in the trees. They seem under strain, almost unable to support themselves. They are rootless, stark against the white gallery walls and polished glass facades. Ai Weiwei stated in the exhibition brochure that he created his trees in an attempt to rediscover their original forest forms. To me, this reads like a misquote.

Perhaps trees are our greatest artists, self-expressing over centuries, becoming ever more complex, growing even in decline and death, and hosting the creative work of thousands of other species. The physical differentiation between individual trees of the same species is huge, the result of their lifelong negotiation with light, space and nutrients. But once dead, trees quickly begin to simplify. They lose hundreds of thousands of twigs in weeks and start to resemble Ai Weiwei's sculptures.

There is an oak tree which borders the playground of my son's old one-room village school, a thousand feet up on the hill. When my son was there the tree was a healthy mature oak, perhaps two centuries old. It had a trunk which leaned and curved out like a bent sickle, and branches which seemed to attempt a counterbalance, reaching back instead of fanning out. My son called it the dancing tree and spoke to it often, as he did with a few trees, this one in particular containing an obvious character that anyone could recognise, though only a child would be brave enough to express it. The little school was closed down after my son had been there only a short time and I didn't visit the place afterwards for perhaps a decade. In that time the oak had died, killed by the creeping disease which continues to consume many old trees in the valley. It had become a wrecked thing, pale, broken, without bark, a ghoulish, still-standing corpse. Its branches appeared as if they had been fetched from elsewhere, dragged from other lands, nailed crudely to the trunk, as if a sculptor had made it as a three-dimensional sketch and then quickly discarded it.

When a tree dies it eventually falls. It leaves a space for young trees to grow into and soon becomes shaded where it softens in the dim light, becoming a host. But the skeleton oaks surrounded by empty fields seem to deter life. Even the birds avoid them. In the early dusk the half-light doesn't collect around them. They stand out, the last shapes we see against the gathering night, like crucifixes.

I'm sitting on a wooden platform fixed between hazel trees, halfway between the canopy and the ground. I built it years ago for my boys and it has long been neglected. The floor planks are twisted and cracked. The handrails are hosts to blue lichens, little crusted pools which are joining together to become a continuous stripe. I'm concerned that the timber will break and send me plummeting, it's happened before. I'm allergic to hazel, both the pollen and nuts. In February each year, when the catkins start to open, my eyes tear up and I sniff and wheeze for months. Every year I say I'm going to cut the trees down. Every year I can't bring myself to do it. In a landscape so bitten down, it's a crime to fell a tree. So the hazels have been left to fan and intertwine. In midsummer the canopy is thick and dark. Up here I'm invisible, surrounded by a hundred thousand serrated hearts. When we first came here twenty years ago the two trees were just a part of the old farm hedge that borders our property and over time we've left them to grow, mostly through neglect. I don't know if they've been allowed to be trees before. They grew quickly once we left them to it and within ten years they were solid enough and tall enough to use for a treehouse. Hazels grow like thought, in a multitude of slender and silvery branches. They bend and break, fall away and are quickly replaced by something similar, but never the same. They're easy to weave into other things.

An hour ago the sky cleared after days of rain. I can see the field beyond the house, the contours of the hill, a slice of sky graduated blue to salmon pink. The grass below is daytime green. But under the canopy night has seeped in. Leaves are shadowy, their etched details filled in, merged together, little clusters of darkness. The negative space created by the leaves is growing. I'm sitting inside it. The Japanese have a word for it – *ma*. The pictograph for this word shows a symbol of the sun through a doorway, the gap where life comes through. The shoot apical meristem of a tree forms the core of each leaf. Within are almost completely featureless cells which have no ageing mechanism. They create eternally a negative space in the stem which makes the forest. *Ma* is present in great Japanese gardens and scroll paintings, in the works of master calligraphers, in Noh theatre, in the minimalist setting of a *chashitsu* and the tea ceremony that takes place within it. It is the nothing that everything emanates from. There is another word in the language that uses *ma* as part of its compound. The word is *ko-no-ma*. It means 'within trees'.

*

The greatest transformation in Earth's biological history cannot be attributed to human beings, but a substance that is too small to be seen. Ribulose-1,5-bisphosphate carboxylase/oxygenase, abbreviated to rubisco, is an enzyme which came into existence over a billion years ago within oceanic algae and which eventually spread on to land via the colonisation of the edges of lakes. It is the substance responsible for bonding inorganic carbon molecules to organic matter in photosynthesis, making life from lifelessness. As algae evolved into early plants, and eventually trees, the enzyme had an ever-greater impact. It sucked carbon out of the atmosphere resulting in oxygenation, and simultaneously triggered the processing of the gathered carbon into silt which was eventually buried deep underground via tectonic movement. This biological process on a miniature scale resulted, over millions of years, in titanic geological and atmospheric changes. The process is made almost miraculous when we take into consideration that rubisco is incredibly inefficient. Most enzymes process around a thousand molecules per second, but rubisco can only achieve three in that time. It is also imprecise and unreliable, being able to attach oxygen molecules as easily as carbon. When this happens it forces the plant cell to perform corrective actions which are costly in terms of energy and resources. For rubisco to be effective it has to be present in huge quantities. It makes up over 50 per cent of all soluble leaf protein and is therefore the most plentiful enzyme in existence. It removed 95 per cent of carbon dioxide in the atmosphere of early Earth, preparing the planet for an explosion of life forms. But as rubisco created life it also destroyed it. Plants and trees proliferated to such an extent that mass cooling of the planet occurred, creating great ice ages with glaciation reaching almost to the tropics, causing mass extinction. Colder and warmer periods oscillated over aeons, wiping out species and creating the conditions for new ones to thrive. These oscillations continue and we should now be heading into a cooling period. Instead, human activity has put this process into reverse.

There was an image circulating on the internet these past weeks that has burned itself into my retinas. It is so powerful that it sits like a translucent curtain in front of everything I look at, the crimson roses that have climbed into my study window, the view over the village to the oaks and the rookery, the mountains across the valley. Over all of it I can see the map of the world, the outlines of all the continents against the oceans. And the flares, each one a forest fire, luminous against the background.

News bulletins have been covering fires in Greece and Italy, and also those in California, which have been an ongoing story for a few years. I have work colleagues in San Francisco who I talk to almost daily. Their families are locked inside for weeks at a time to keep out of the smoke from nearby blazes, the air pollution at deadly levels. On the map the brightest areas are in Africa. The whole of the Congo seems to be burning, Central and East Africa lit up, Zambia, Angola, Tanzania, Kenya. There are fires in places where it is now winter, in Australia, New Zealand, Patagonia. Even in the cold and wet north, in Siberia, Iceland and Northern Canada, there are blazes seemingly everywhere. So far this year wildfires have emitted six gigatons of carbon dioxide, more than the industrial emissions of Europe. All the wild mammals on Earth collectively weigh one gigaton.

I zoom into the wildfires of Kenya. As the image is magnified the clustered red dots start to separate and scatter, getting smaller. Most of the fires cover tens or hundreds of acres, with large areas in between. It makes me feel slightly better. I look up from the screen, out of my window, across the fields. It's going to rain, the blue gaps in the sky closing, the light fading a little. I stand up and walk out into the garden. There are house martins chittering high up, a single buzzard higher still, stirring the soup of the clouds. I watch it as it drifts northwards towards a distant ridge which is covered in heather and bilberry, a grouse moor being recreated after years of quiet neglect by the previous landowner. Soon the gamekeepers will be burning off old heather to create new growth for the grouse to feed on. When they start a burn it sometimes last days. I've driven home from work after dark to see orange light like a second sunset haloing the ridge. It's an ancient image for us humans who long ago created landscapes like this by fire. They must have been spectacular, the scenes we created by burning the trees, whole valleys lit up, the birds and insects swirling overhead with the fiery embers, our ancestors watching the forests shatter and go down.

*

A decade ago it was thought that rainfall was caused almost wholly by evaporation from the oceans, but several studies have emerged since demonstrating that precipitation from the oceans carries inland for only a few hundred miles. Trees carry the rest. A single mature tree can transpire up to a hundred gallons of water every day. Eighty per cent of the rainfall in China originates not in the Pacific Ocean or China Seas, but in the north Atlantic. It is carried across the Eurasian continent by the forests of Scandinavia and Siberia where it is recycled several times, trees pulling rainwater from the soil up into their leaves where it is released back into the air via their pores. Above these forests are invisible rivers flowing through the sky. They are far longer than any of the great terrestrial rivers and hold more water. Other studies have demonstrated that the process of evaporation and condensation above the forests creates a biotic pump, causing changes in air pressure in the vertical and horizontal planes that lead to the creation of winds which push the sky rivers across continents. Trees create the rains and trees create the winds to move the rains.

When forests are cut down for crops, sky rivers start to dry up and the winds die. Desertification begins. The great desert depressions in the arid interior of Australia were once huge lakes, fed by monsoons. Lake Eyre contained ten thousand square kilometres of fresh water. Now it is a salt pan most of the time. There are no climatic explanations for the drying out of the Australian interior forty-five thousand years ago, no sudden warming. But at that time humans arrived on the continent, burning forests to create pasture. As the trees burned transpiration ceased, the sky rivers disappeared and a desert was created. Australian forests continue to be destroyed. In the past 50 years 130,000 square kilometres of forest on the west coast have been cut down and transformed into wheat fields. These crops are now being decimated by droughts. Much of Europe would be arid but for the huge forests of Russia and the sky rivers which transport the rains westward over them. These forests are being felled faster than in any other part of the world and the wildfires that now occur frequently have become so huge that Russian authorities have given up trying to control them.

*

Our youngest son Lewis was unhappy to be brought into the world. He cried continually, his tiny face scrunched and purple, his little fists knotted. No amount of rocking and cooing would calm him down. The only response I know to a crisis is to walk, the greater the upset the further the distance. So each time he began wailing I strapped him into the baby carrier and set out. He would continue to scream for the first few miles while I walked up the lanes and across open fields, until I reached John's wood. Then, under the cover of the trees, the tension in him started to ease, the screams turning to sobs, to deep, even breaths, to a single sigh. His deep blue eyes, which had been clamped slits, slowly opened. Babies seem to hover on the threshold of life for a while after they are born, as if they see two worlds graduating into each other, like day and night. Lewis was born two days before the summer solstice, at the time when the daylight glare is brightest. Perhaps the light frightened him as it streamed in through the windows across the bare hills. But once he was beneath the trees he was happy. The graduated translucence and the soothing leaf colours that changed as we walked below the canopy brought with them a womb-like calm. He would stare up at the gently rocking canopy, taking it all in, little primate, evolved from the twilight world of the forest. Years later he still loves the woods. He goes out most days, just before dark, to walk under the trees, gazing up at what Henry David Thoreau termed 'chandeliers of darkness'.

Hypersensitivity runs in the family. I was an anxiety-ridden child, easily upset by the slightest thing. Infant and middle schools were a trial. It was common back then for teachers to shout and corporal punishment was the norm – rulers, shoes and canes used daily on our hands and backsides. I was also deeply introverted and didn't make friends easily. The result was that I was often sick, the thought of entering the school gates making my stomach churn. My anxiety made it difficult to concentrate and I spent a lot of my time staring out of windows instead of at blackboards, trying to tune out of the classroom environment. I believe that, over the years, this habit turned into an attention disorder which I still struggle with today. I find it hard to concentrate for extended periods of time and conversations are always difficult as I often lose the thread or miss what others are saying. But my sensitivity seems to have worked in the opposite way concerning the other-than-human environment, tuning in rather than out. Most children seem to have a deep sense of connection with nature when very young which falls away as they reach their teens. It didn't happen to me, my connection deepened as I got older. Witnessing the ongoing devastation in the natural world during my lifetime has resulted in an emotional wound which is permanently raw. There are times in these hills when I feel like I'm living in a vast graveyard, the sense of loss becomes overwhelming.

On 21 January 1856, a great elm tree was felled in the town of Concord, Massachusetts, after the owner of the tree grew concerned about a crack in a branch which had been creaking in a storm. Present for the felling was Henry David Thoreau, who wrote about it in his journal. That day's entry, when the tree was hauled to the ground, was filled with observations of the tree's size and girth, its approximate age and condition. He described a fruit bush which had been growing in its upper branches and a brick which had been encased by the elm's trunk. On 22 January, his tone changed and he recorded that he had revisited the prone tree to say a eulogy for it, drowned out by the sound of axes from the army of men who were now hacking the tree into firewood. His lines are full of praise for the tree and for the other old elms of the town, which he regarded as ancient members of the community and honourable citizens. 'A fragment of their bark is worth the backs of all the politicians in the union,' he wrote on 24 January. The cutting down of possibly the oldest member of that community he regarded as sacrilegious and he bemoaned the fact that only he was there to honour the passing of the ancient being. He was writing at a time when Concord was already abandoning its two-centuries-old agricultural tradition and embracing the industrial world, symbolised by the arrival of the railway. Farmers in the area were quitting their land and moving to the cities. Their fields, created by the felling and burning of the ancient wildwood, were reforesting.

Thoreau understood forest regeneration and studied it closely. He coined the term 'succession' and gave a lecture about it which was widely disseminated. His work contributed to the understanding of woodland management and the life cycle of trees. Though his acute observations were those of an experienced naturalist and scientist, his writings on trees also contained a deeply felt poetic sensibility. One of his greatest works is the posthumously published essay 'Autumnal Tints', first published in the October 1862 issue of *The Atlantic* magazine. The piece follows the procession of autumn through tree and plant species, beginning with the purple grasses and red maple, which first transform in August and September. It then progresses through elm, sugar maple, and finally scarlet oak, which changes colour late, as autumn fuses with winter. Along the way he describes in close detail the myriad colours and patterns he encounters, the huge drifts of leaves he walks through, even how the little waterway he travels on in his small boat is transformed in the autumn to a river of leaves. His transcendent descriptions of oak trees create images of headlands, peninsulas and narrow coves within a single leaf. A thread running through the whole essay examines death in the natural world. Thoreau believed that leaves provide an example to us. They are at their most beautiful in the days before they fall and when they do finally detach from the tree they become part of the soil, enriching the lives that follow. 'How beautifully they go to their graves!' he wrote. '... They teach us how to die.'

*

The wild world is a place of constant and sometimes rapid transformation. Landmarks disappear in an instant. Mountains collapse, rents in rocks appear and reveal caves the size of cathedrals which later flood or fold back on themselves and become rubble. Islands boil out of the sea. Species that have seen out multiple ice ages go suddenly extinct. They're here and then they're gone. In 2006, the remains of a forest were found a hundred metres below ground in the Vermilion Grove coal mine in Illinois. Fossil plants and trees are commonly found in coal shale, but they are fragmentary, usually only a few metres square. After the removal of these particular coal deposits surveyors found giant fossils of tree roots, fallen trunks and an array of species in spectacular detail which stretched several square kilometres into the mine's tunnels. It is now thought that the forest reaches a hundred kilometres into the earth. A part of it shows the path of a river as wide as the Mississippi. The forest had been preserved intact by rapid flooding which buried trees alive, masses of silt pouring in over a period of a few days. The water level rose at least thirty metres in that time, higher than the highest trees. The tallest trees were lycopsids, which resembled poles, their leaves tightly covering the trunk like green scales. Only towards the end of their lives did these trees produce fanned branches at their crowns, an adaptation which allowed the dispersal of spores across the widest area possible. Below this thin canopy grew smaller species like tree ferns, seed ferns, calamites and cordaites. The forest now exists as an etched print on the ceiling of a labyrinth, an underbelly view of the planet's early imaginings. It hides below the pitch dark of the present where vast amounts of carbon, removed from the atmosphere by rubisco over millions of years, has been dug out and burned in a geological second, flipping the atmosphere into its current warming state, creating storms which wipe out the miracles of the world in an instant.

The Vermilion Grove mine once produced over a million tons of coal each year, but was decommissioned when the operation became unprofitable. The land around it, including the spoil heaps and pools, were eventually reclaimed. The water was cleaned and the coal mixed with lime to deacidify it before topsoil was used to cap the area. Afterwards crops were planted on the reclaimed land and fish stocks added to the now clean pools. Wildlife returned to the area. The mine owner, Peabody Energy, subsequently won an environmental award for the project. In 2021, after years of unprofitability and almost bankruptcy, Peabody, owner of the world's biggest operational coal mine at Rochelle in Wyoming, posted a record final-quarter net income of $513 million dollars, up from a loss of $129 million dollars the year before. This was due to the increase in prices for natural gas and the subsequent switchover of some power stations back to coal, despite a global political commitment to phase out the use of this most dangerous of carbon sources. Peabody estimated a 20 per cent increase in demand in 2022.

*

All the way here, travelling for two hours through the steep-sided valleys of Mid Wales, I've seen fringes of trees along thin, winding rivers. Above them, rising into the sky, blocking out the low morning sun and prolonging the dawn, are smooth green slopes, speckled with white dots, the thousands of sheep that graze every hill that isn't shadowed with a conifer plantation. Here and there, taking up a minuscule proportion of the landscape, there have been oak woods, tiny remnants of the old forest.

It's been a while since I came this way and in that time many of the big conifer plantations have been felled. Whole hillsides have been razored down to stubble or piled with tree debris. Many have been replanted, leaving uniform columns and rows of toy Christmas trees. Now I'm at the edge of the sea, on Europe's Atlantic fringe, standing in a rainforest that is five thousand years old. Oak, pine, birch, willow, hazel, these are the main species here. It's a forest that, at high tide, you can swim above, peering down into the blue twilight at the tops of the trees, or diving down to touch the boles, branches and roots. The old name for this place is Cantre'r Gwaelod (The Lowland Hundred) and there are legends associated with it, antediluvian stories of a wide and rich landscape walled off from the sea which was accidentally and tragically flooded thousands of years ago. The legends are partly true. After the last glaciation a high bar of stones and sand formed a few kilometres west of here, protecting a fresh-water lagoon and an area of fenland which quickly became colonised by the trees that dominated further inland. For two thousand years a temperate rainforest grew here. Then the sandbar began to shift east and the area was breached by the sea. The forest drowned. The remains of the trees were buried and preserved in a deep layer of peat, then covered with sand. In recent years, increasingly powerful storms have removed the layers of sand and now the forest is visible again, stretching four kilometres south from the Dyfi Estuary.

It is low tide; stones, shells, sand and water sparking. I'm crouching over a tapering pine bole, shaped like the cone of a volcano. Its growth rings are clear and easy to count, almost a hundred of them, the outer rings smoothed and sanded by the tide, the inner rings toothed and feathered. Thick roots twist away from the bole, through a thick layer of peat impregnated with twigs and debris, then dig into the sand. In the hollows and creases of the tree remains there are white pebbles, shells, aprons of green seaweed. The bole is drying in the sun, exposed heartwood pale brown to cream, bark copper bronze. The tree has been here for four thousand years. Looking north the black stumps stretch out of sight. People are walking in between them, taking pictures of each other with their phones, their dogs sniffing the stumps, kids kicking footballs against them, climbing and jumping over them. It's a playground and a monument. It was also once a hunting and foraging ground. Footprints have been discovered in the peat, as have antler tools, flints and struts that propped up walkways and platforms. There are many other traces of our ancestors here which will never be discovered; archaeologists and paleobiologists get little time to work on the site, restricted by the tides and seasons. The forest appears and disappears, almost mythically. Sand washes in with each tide and covers some of the remains. Storms scour the sand away, revealing the trees again, each time a little less than the last. People travel long distances to see the spectacle, hoping for weather like this, the glare of a warm day, the black of the forest, the white of the beach.

*

At the edge of John's wood is a patch of ground which has been kept as grass. Around the edge is a circular path made by horses' hooves years ago. Inside the circle the turf gives way to oak saplings each year, hundreds of them, a bristle garden. For now the saplings are being cut back in the winter to keep the space open, but eventually they'll take over and the wood will expand further. All a forest requires to expand is a little neglect. The etymology of the word traces to a variant of the Latin word *neclegere*, which is a composite of two Proto-Indo-European words: *ne-*, meaning 'not', and *leg-*, meaning 'to gather'.

This area marks the edge of the Devensian ice sheet. The Black Mountains rising on the other side of the valley are obvious glacier-created forms, their moraines still visible in places. It's easy to imagine the valley hosting the terminus of a glacier calving into the beginnings of the river, the face of the ice sheet blue, holding the glare of a slowly warming sun. At its perimeter there would have been stony ground, thinly and sporadically coated with bryophytes and mosses. Perhaps, here and there, a dwarf willow or juniper tree would start to grow, barely surviving in the hostile environment, but still spraying out their seeds on to the ground. Twilight over the ice must have made this valley glow, the receding light, like the ice itself, holding on, penetrating and refracting in the frozen layers, a phosphorescence lingering to the edge of night. But as the ice melted and the trees advanced another visual spectacle emerged, a green dawn. The glare over the scraped land faded. It was scribbled out, woven over, entangled. The forest headed north like a giant ark, bringing with it a host of species. Eventually it would bring wolves, beavers, bears, goshawks.

I'm out with the dogs in John's wood early in the evening. Our young spaniel bounces through the tangled understorey then runs through tunnels she's made in the bracken on previous visits. Our old Labrador watches her then trots away to find her own entertainment, snuffling around abandoned rabbit holes. I'm standing with my head back watching the light change beneath two oak trees, debating if I'm brave enough to climb them now and wondering how much they've grown since the last time I climbed them a decade ago. I've been coming to this wood for twenty years, almost half its lifetime, and almost half mine. The oaks must have grown several metres in that time. The place is darker than it used to be, more entangled. New species have arrived: dog rose, wild honeysuckle, field maple, elder, rowan. They creep into the spaces between the more mature trees and grow, almost invisibly. Beside the path, in a line along the edge of the lane, is a stand of Scots pines, the highest of which is perhaps thirty metres tall. Beneath them it is always dark, the ground cushioned with a deep layer of fallen needles. It is from their shadowed branches that a shriek now breaks, ricocheting like a gunshot, so loud it makes me flinch. A winged shape I cannot identify rushes overhead. I can just make out its vague form, moving fast, skeltering from the wood. The shriek turns to a high-pitched yammer, an ululation two octaves above any sound a human could make. The last half-note is overlapped by the barking dogs as they appear from the undergrowth, sprinting down the path full tilt, giving chase to the thing. They have never heard this sound before, and nor have I. I'm stunned and shining. I think we've just encountered a goshawk. I've been told they nest locally, probably in the plantation down the hill where it is darker, quieter, more secretive. They come here to hunt in the more open spaces between the trees. There must have been times they've perched above me in the high branches when I've shuffled past, elsewhere, eyes to the ground, my mind caught in a gyre of thoughts.

Goshawks are one of the few wildlife success stories in Wales. They became locally extinct in the nineteenth century, but have made a comeback in recent decades. Their recovery is not as well publicised as that of red kites, perhaps because the goshawks are so hard to find, living in the twilight of remnant woods and the almost night of plantations. Witnessing one is a mini miracle. I'm staring at the contrail of its passing, my blood pumping, whirling thoughts vaporised in an instant. My dogs have become wolves.

At this time of day, fifty years ago, ponies would start their descent from the top of the hill, walking down the lanes and tracks, ripping at the uncut grasses on the verges, making their way here to graze in the scattered spaces between thick growths of gorse and brambles. The herd cropped the thin grass down and moved on, sometimes ending up in the churchyard in the village below where the grass was lush between graves. There is a photograph of the little common from that time. It is almost bone bare with just a few thorn trees visible. Soon after the picture was taken a cattle grid was installed and the ponies could no longer range freely. At the same time the local farmers decided not to graze their sheep here as the area was too small and the ground too infested with brambles and bracken. The little common began to return to woodland under John's care.

Bracken is a pioneer species. Wherever it grows eventually turns to woodland if left. Seeds dropped by birds turn into saplings and push through the tangled, spiky undergrowth that protects them while they're fragile. The bracken shelters the new roots, holding moisture for them. As the saplings turn to trees the ground becomes shaded below them. Slowly the bracken thins and makes way. This process is clear to see here. Where the tree canopy is dense there is little bracken now, the ground colonised by many species of fungi. The trees have thrived and other plant species have returned: bluebell, goat willow, forget-me-not, trefoil, bugloss, dead-nettle, dog's mercury, celandine, stitchwort, cuckooflower. With them came insects and birds. Eventually the goshawks arrived.

Over the same period of time that John's wood grew, much

of the forested land on Earth has been cut and burned back, the period when Western civilisation ramped up its destruction of Earth and turned the Holocene into the Anthropocene. It took humans ten thousand years to destroy half of Earth's forests, the whole of our history since the invention of agriculture. It has taken us less than a century to destroy most of the other half. In that time we've let in the light on an area of land twice the size of the United States, cutting off all the species and wild processes that the trees hosted, even the transportation of rain. Many of these areas have transformed, or are transforming, into desert.

There are other places like John's wood here and there in the valley, little patches of land which have been neglected or allowed to regrow under the stewardship of individuals who perhaps view the land around them as part of the community. Only two miles away another wood has regrown on a former sheep common. The trees are still immature, the species not as diverse, but, in time and if left, it will grow into another miniature wildwood. Perhaps the fields between the two woods will also be left to the wild some day, and they will connect, come back to life and slowly spread a green twilight over the valley as they once did. Eventually we could call it a rainforest.

THE CHURCH AND THE ISLAND

They are stalking, creeping, stilting through treacle mud at low tide, water lapping their bony feet, the water of the Atlantic, of the Severn, the Avon, the Wye. There are over a hundred strung out in lines, in loose pairs, in trios. Above them are the great concrete steeples and arcs of a suspension bridge spanning the mile-wide river mouth, which hums with engine noise, drowning their calls. They were feeding from this shore when humans first came to this place, before we built our first enclosures of wood and stone, our stone towers, our bridges of steel and concrete.

They've survived months of storms and cold. Soon they'll be on the move, back to the uplands and river meadows. The rush hour is over and now there is a lull in the traffic overhead. Their fluting calls ring across the water in the brief quiet, the long arc of their songs. Perhaps their calls led our ancestors to shape flutes from river reeds, to create the music of worship. Their name in old Welsh means 'mountain flute'. They are creatures of St Beuno, who could raise the dead, who could walk on water. It is said that he was crossing a stretch of water like this, singing his prayers, when he dropped his book of sermons into the water. When he reached the shore he saw a curlew standing on the book, guarding it for him. As an act of reciprocation he prayed to God to hide their nests and eggs so no creature could find them, though they were built on the ground. For centuries the saint's request kept the birds from harm, but now saints and their prayers are no longer remembered. The curlews are disappearing from the rivers and mountains of Wales. Each year more pairs fail to breed. One of those pairs are here now, oblivious to their future. In a few days they will fly north, forty miles to a bare-sided hill where they will mate in sight of a church shadowed by yew trees. Other birds will follow the river upstream to a valley of rich meadows beside the water. They will find fields left uncut through spring. They'll nest in peace and raise their young. There will be an old boat moored next to one of these fields. Inside it a man will be listening to their dusk calls while he tries to shape a prayer.

*

The storm is growing, the sky hammered lead. On the dim-lit lane that climbs the ridge water is pooling in potholes. The lane runs over a ford which is a foot deep in fast sliding water. There is a badly painted sign for the church screwed to an old, broken gate. A piece of frayed string is tied to a metal post to keep the gate closed. I unfasten it, step through and I'm walking across a sheep-shitty field with lambs running from me as if they'd never witnessed a human being. The wind hits with full force as it scours the upslope. At the far end of the field is a copse of beeches still in their winter bones, and beneath them the thick dark of many yews almost obscuring the walls and roof of the church. Not long ago this place served a population who worked the land entirely by hand, but the close-knit interdependence of the community was replaced by the efficiency of machines. The people are gone, the machines remain. Every nearby farm seems to have its own graveyard of rusting metal: old tractors, threshers, seed drills. They have been upgraded and replaced by bigger, faster machines, as the farm workers before them were. There is a large farmhouse down the slope from the church, a half-ruin, huge barns with bitten-out tin roofs and tumbling walls. The yard holds a small herd of black cattle, barn-housed all winter. They'll be in the fields soon, once these winds and the cold nights wane, when the grass starts to grow. For now they remain locked up, plastered in their own dung, forlorn.

The church is still functioning. There are services held here twice a month, though I doubt if more than a handful of people come to them. The only sign that the place is still used is a recent grave at the entrance to the churchyard with its shining, machine-polished headstone. Next to it is a bouquet of fresh flowers placed in an urn, together with a collection of plastic ornaments. It is surrounded by ancient headstones, leaning like drunks, coated with green, orange and white lichens, each one a garden. The ground around the church has heaved and bulged. It is knuckled with the roots of yews, one tree at least five hundred years old. Beneath their canopies is a permanent, webbed twilight. Between the roots and among the graves the ground is thick with weeds and wildflowers, nettle and bluebell, stitchwort, cuckooflower, wood violet. A tide of golden saxifrage runs right up to the walls. The untended graveyards of the uplands have become its wildest spaces.

The first time I visited the tiny St David's Church at Llandewi Fach, a remote upland hamlet, there was a faded and foxed sheet of information on the door, written by hand, almost illegible, outlining the history of the place. It was originally a hermitage, founded possibly in the sixth century by a follower of St David. In the early Celtic Church many monks became hermits, a way of life that was seen as a form of martyrdom. There were three levels of martyrdom: red, green and white. Red martyrdom could only be achieved through torture and death in the manner of Christ and his apostles. Green or blue martyrdom was a lesser form requiring devotees to refrain from many activities which were seen as sinful. White martyrdom required exile, across the sea or to remote areas, as well as strict asceticism. David, the most famous of Welsh saints, lived on a barren peninsula where the cathedral built in his name and the palatial monastery built after his death now stand. David's asceticism is well documented. The community of monks he gathered around him were forbidden all luxuries and labour-saving tools. They were even required to pull their own ploughs. David himself regularly stood up to his neck in the cold winter sea for long periods of penitence. His ability to withstand such tribulations enabled him to carry out acts of thaumaturgy which became legend. He cured the blind and sick, resurrected the dead, and made hills rise from flat fields so he could address congregations.

One of St David's devotees could have chosen white martyrdom and travelled here to found the church in his name, deep in the then-remote forest that covered most of the Welsh borders. His bones may lie beneath the sandstone floor of the church, or in the graveyard, a brittle scapula, a femur, a toothless skull revealing the severity of his asceticism. Perhaps his remains are layered with the bones of the wolves and beavers, lynxes and wild cats that could have existed here at that time.

Asceticism in the West originated in ancient Greece, where abstinence from some foods, drinks and activities like sexual intercourse, which were known to sap energy from the body, was originally practised by athletes and soldiers in periods before competition or battle. Abstinence was believed to assist the body to achieve the peak of physical performance. The practice was then adopted by Stoics and Sophists, who used it to purify not the body, but the soul. It spread into Christian culture in the centuries after the death of Christ when monasteries were founded in the harshest areas of the Egyptian desert.

The monk Evagrius Ponticus is still a revered figure in the Eastern Church, though his name is almost unknown in the West. He was an intellectual who became a monk and who created a large collection of theological and philosophical writings in the form of letters, theses, brief sayings and proverbs. His 'eight evil thoughts' are possibly the origin of the seven deadly sins. In his best-known work, the *Praktikos*, Evagrius invented a system to combat the sins, which each derived from a thought emanating under the influence of a demon. Demons were figures who existed in physical form, but who were only faintly visible, even to the best-trained eye. They could easily infiltrate the mind and embed thoughts that would lead inevitably to an act of sin, forcing the ascetic away from the true path.

Evagrius listed all the methods via which a demonically implanted thought could be recognised. Each sinful projection was to be combatted by a counter-thought, usually in the form of the repetition of a prayer or psalm, in an attempt to banish the demon and subdue the passions. The *Praktikos* goes into lengthy detail about thought processes and resembles some modern psychological techniques like cognitive behavioural therapy in its remedial methods. It also predates Jung's theory of the shadow self by fifteen centuries.

Evagrian knowledge is tactical, combative. It describes hierarchies of demons and outlines manoeuvres with which to battle them. These manoeuvres can be physical as well as mental. Evagrius recommended weeping for days at a time as the highest act of asceticism. He also practised harsh physical methods and was known, like St David, to immerse himself in water on the coldest days to counteract thoughts of fornication, which were said to afflict him continuously. Evagrius was a huge influence on Christian asceticism in the medieval period and his writings fed into a mythology of suffering which was further enhanced by places, deserts and inhospitable wildernesses where the ascetic would be afflicted not only by their internal thoughts and passions, but also by the demons who dwelled in those places.

Some ascetics were known to have asked for death without burial or blessing, for their bodies to be left lying where they expired or to be thrown out of the monastery into a ditch to be consumed by scavengers. It was the ultimate demonstration of non-attachment to the flesh. As death approached a brother monk, other monks would eagerly gather around while his mind was still active, asking urgent questions: were the gates of heaven open for him, had his life of hardship earned him a place in paradise, had he achieved apocatastasis, restoration to the primordial, sinless condition?

It is unknown how the hermit who inhabited this place where the church now stands lived his life, but it was likely inspired by the monks of the Egyptian desert and by the teachings of Evagrius. The forest that is now long gone was a wilderness, a difficult place to survive, and the perfect place to practise hermetic asceticism. He would have spent his time here in combat with himself, observing every thought, duelling it with a counter-thought. He was self-hating, self-obsessed, standing for days in prayer until his ankles thickened and his feet bled, attempting to defeat the body and feeling only the pain of the body.

An iron hook serves as a latch. I lift it with difficulty and push the heavy door, which slides open. A slow light bleeds from the graveyard into the church interior, barely touching the shadows, which are solid, three-dimensional. You could almost lift them.

It is always dusk in here. Though the windows are large they are smoked with grime, greened with mould, and tapping the glass are the hanging yew trees, woven tight.

On one of my first trips to upland Wales I climbed a bleak hill, late in the day, to a dilapidated sheepfold in order to shelter from a squall twisting into the valley. Behind the broken walls, beneath a metal roof, were the rotted remains of a sheep, a wool-coated skeleton, a void-eyed skull separated from the body. As I bent to look, the farmer came down the field in his Land Rover and I collapsed to the ground, pressing myself hard against the wall, lying on the bones. The atmosphere of the place made me feel like a thief, an invader on his land. I hid, as if for my survival. I waited long after the putter of the engine had faded back to birdsong before I conjured the courage to peer out. I get the same sensation here sometimes, I'm unwelcome, the church and its ghosts want me gone. It feels wrong to even sit at a pew, as if there are already people sitting there, or at least that their places are reserved. I stand with my camera and notebook resting on top of the old organ, scribbling at speed.

Everything in here is monotone: faded stone, faded wood, faded brass. Except for two bouquets of plastic flowers, one propped on a windowsill, the other on the hearth of an open fireplace, both shockingly gaudy and out of place. On the pale, plastered walls there are overlaid stripes of cast shade, the verticals of candlesticks, diagonals of leaded window frames, finger weaves of branches, layer on layer, faintly moving over each other. The room clings to its adumbrations. Behind the shadows are deep cracks in the plaster, black streaks of mildew. On the floors wide oak boards are spattered with old wax. I lift the lid on the organ keyboard. The keys are made from bone that has split and delaminated. I press a couple. A deadened thump precedes the silence it rings from the room.

Sound changes at twilight. An atmosphere descends colouring bird calls, voices, the hiss of tyres. In the day there is a symphony of sound, if we are lucky enough to be in the right place, a cacophony otherwise. At dusk the symphony becomes a concerto. It simplifies. We hear the notes, bell clear. A curlew call at dusk generates a wave of quiet around it that can make the air temperature drop. Inside this church, at any time of day, the sounds of the outside world are mediated by stone, deadened to muffled semitones. Outside there is a flock of noisy jackdaws, their calls as hard as their shapes against the sky. But in here the edges of each cracked note are feathered. There are also blue tits and great tits nesting in the churchyard, sparrows, blackbirds. Their higher-pitched calls are softened and blurred against the hush of the wind, which seems far away.

The windows are broken, some of the diamonds of glass cracked or missing. On the stone sills are placed dusty vases, oil lanterns, half-melted candles standing in wax pools. Cobwebs have been built and rebuilt, as dense as birds' nests in places, like tattered curtains in others. They ruffle and swing against the broken glass. In the window next to the oak door I can see the outline of a butterfly caught inside a thick web. I step between the pews and lean in to get a better look. Its colours are faded to dust grey but I can just see its markings, a red admiral. It must have flown in through one of the broken panes and got caught. Many spiders have weak jaws. They are unable to chew the tougher parts of their prey and therefore pierce two holes with their hollow fangs and inject venom mixed with digestive enzymes. This liquidises the internal organs and musculature, which can then be sucked out of the body. What remains of the red admiral are its faded wings, its emptied thorax and abdomen. Though butterflies are not mentioned in the Bible they have become a symbol of the Resurrection. At Easter, paper or fabric butterflies are often used as decorations, sometimes mounted on the nails of the cross. Their metamorphic life cycle reflects that of Christ. They die and are reborn, they ascend. In the case of this butterfly, caught in the web, an additional phase has been added to its metamorphosis, a dissolution and withering to the dry grey of a church interior.

There is room for one hundred and fifty people in here, five to each pew with standing room at the back. At the front of the pews is an oak pulpit with two worn steps up to it. Behind that is an altar with a table draped in cloth, backed with red curtains. There is no cross, but it was there once, the focus of the congregation, symbol of our sins and the promise of life beyond this life. The faithful came here each week to be shut in for a few hours of sensory deprivation in exchange for eternity in paradise.

*

Not far from here is another church built into a high hill, associated with Cynog, one of the storied Celtic saints. His legend tells of the time when Cynog's fellow monks tired of the hardships he demanded and set upon him as he walked up to his mountain home from the fields at dusk. They beat him to death and cut off his head. The saint then stood up and walked off, carrying his head down the hill to find a better place to rest. Perhaps he chose the yew tree which now stands in the churchyard, which was already there in his day.

The Defynnog Yew has stood for at least fifteen hundred years and is believed by some to be up to five thousand years old. Its bole is so huge that there are steps into it and a path leading through. A sacred golden bough grows from it. It occupies a quiet corner of a graveyard which contains a standing stone with a Roman and Ogham inscription. Inside the church is a font carved in the Saxon era. The place has been a ritual centre for millennia. There are few records of pre-Christian religious practices involving yew trees but it is presumed that they were used as gathering places. The trees with their renowned longevity and lethally poisonous needles were symbols of life and death. The ritual of putting a yew branch into a coffin with the body of the deceased was documented very recently and may still be practised in upland Wales.

The tree, though huge, seems able to vanish within its own shadows. On a recent visit, a morning of hard frost, I sat inside the trunk watching the sun slowly burn the blue-white-coated weeds and turf back to green as it travelled low over the mountain. Several visitors came to the churchyard, presumably to see the tree, wandering slowly up and down the paths. None found it. It overhangs to the ground, draws a curtain around itself. It spends its days projecting a pointillist twilight over the theatre of its interior, a wind tremor going through its branches and needles. Its lifespan contains perhaps the whole Christian era, the waning of the Welsh language, British imperialism and the industrial revolution. If left in peace it will outlive the information age and all our furious technologies.

*

There is a church at the foot of the Black Mountains which I visit often, perhaps the most remote of all the churches in the area. The lane leading to the place runs through an old farm which has changed little in centuries. A 1950s tractor, a broken Daihatsu and the rusted-out corrugated roofs on the barns are the only signs of the industrial revolution. Black cattle stare from stone pens. A miserly wisp of woodsmoke rises from the chimney. I imagine someone bent, shivering in front of the hearth, feeding it damp, popping sticks. Though the surrounding land is emerald green you still sense ruin there. I walk through the farmyard as quickly as possible, feeling unwelcome, not by the inhabitants, but by the stones of the place.

Of all the churches in these hills it is the only one I know which does not have a yew tree inside the grounds. Instead it stands beyond the graveyard wall, opposite the entrance, on a platform of earth like a makeshift stage. The yew is known as the whipping tree. Two holes have been bored into it, terminating as they reach the hollow of the tree's inner trunk. Put your arms inside and you can feel a smooth section of new growth, an inner root which will eventually replace the original trunk and give the tree a second existence. By then perhaps the memories of what people did here will have faded away.

> It is ordered that William George, who was convicted of Petit Larceny be confined to Hard Labour in the House of Correction for the Term of Three Months and on the Saturday immediately before the Expiration of his Confinement to be Publicly whipped for the space of Half an Hour until his Body be Bloody.

The whipping was usually dealt out by the church warden, who was paid for the work. Most of the punished crimes were committed by the desperately poor. One recorded case was for the stealing of a pile of rags. Women were stripped to the waist the same as men. Some were walked through the village after the whipping took place so that people could see their bleeding wounds.

> It is ordered that Elizabeth Reece, who was convicted of Felony at this Quarter Sessions be brought up at the Hour of Twelve o'Clock at Noon on Saturday, there to receive Fifty Lashes with a Cat of Nine Tails on her Bare Back and that a minute elapse between every stroke and then be discharged.

Terror management theory is a psychological theory based on the work of the cultural anthropologist Ernest Becker, who attempted to justify human behaviour in terms of the ongoing awareness of death. He believed that our world view is shaped in order to protect ourselves from the meaninglessness of a life that will inevitably and randomly end. We seek control over the uncontrollable by inventing meaning in the form of rigid social codes and beliefs. The more the idea of death is salient, the more extremely we attach ourselves to these beliefs and punish those who appear to question them. Many experiments have been undertaken to support the theory. One involved twenty-two municipal court judges in Arizona who were asked to make decisions on the bail of a woman who had been charged with prostitution. Half of the judges were asked to read the case notes and give an amount. The notes given to the other eleven judges came with a questionnaire which asked them to imagine their own deaths and how that made them feel. The control group on average set a bond of fifty dollars, normal for the crime. The group who had been asked to think about their own deaths set an average bond ten times higher.

The whipping tree was surrounded by the graves of the recently deceased, some of them the children and partners of parishioners, the whipping carried out by the same people who had conducted their funerals and buried their bodies. The church was probably founded as a hermitage, home to another martyr who came here to punish himself. Centuries have passed since the tree was last used, enough time for its trunk to heal. But people have been vigilant in their tending to it, cutting back new growth so that the holes for the victims' arms do not disappear, holding on to the memory of what happened here, though their ancestors occupy the graves which have long been neglected.

*

I spent a short time earlier in my life as a practising Christian. I was eighteen and at a sixth form college I hated. Many of my friends had decided that further education was not for them and had instead gone to work in the factories and mines that were still in operation then. I was lonely and studying subjects I had no interest in, and no ability at. I was floundering, sitting in classrooms surrounded by kids who seemed brighter than me and were certainly better educated. I remember trying to decipher equations on blackboards which I had no comprehension of, the fear and bewilderment rising in me to panic levels. I was too introverted and ashamed to ask for help from the teachers, so I failed every test, getting bottom marks each time. In the end I dropped all my academic subjects and took easier alternatives, which I also eventually failed. I sank into a period of depression.

I was invited to visit a chapel one evening by a friend and a few hours later sat next to him on a pew listening to him, and many other people, talking in tongues. This loud glossolalia sounded to my ignorant ears like a language communicated by the divine. I then spent almost a year trying to connect with the source of that mystery. I dabbled with asceticism, giving up alcohol, sex, swearing,

television, music and books. I read the New Testament over and over and attended church meetings twice a week. I prayed every night, long into the night, in an attempt, like Evagrius, to banish my demons, fending off thoughts and temptations that came drifting in from the part of me that just wanted to be a teenager. The thoughts were parried, confronted, banished. They rebounded, amplified, fought back. I tried more severe methods, starting with a full submersion baptism in a plastic tub, watched by a baying audience of believers. Periods without sleep followed, cold showers, complete withdrawal from all my friends. Nothing worked. My precariously held faith collapsed and my failure at self-denial led me back into the world. Eventually, through a series of accidents and synchronicities, I found that art, not religion, was my salvation. What I carry with me from that experience is a vague sense of loss which comes from the absence of the divine. A part of me continually hopes for experiences of the numinous. The closest I ever get is at twilight on a high hill, listening to the calls of curlews.

I don't remember praying during the time of Julia's illness. For most of it I was caught up in the whirlwind of daily chores and obligations. There was always something to do, something to arrange, appointments to attend, work deadlines to somehow meet despite the chaos that reigned at home. There were a few months after Julia's radiotherapy treatment when things calmed down a little and she seemed to be recovering. But on a morning when I'd just arrived at work I got a phone call from her telling me she couldn't breathe. An ambulance was called and by the time I got to the hospital she'd been admitted to a ward and was having X-rays and multiple tests. Her blood glucose was four times higher than normal and there were shadows on her lungs. Eventually diabetes was diagnosed, but the breathing difficulties were caused by pulmonary embolisms, with several blood clots present. At the time neither of us knew how dangerous the condition was. There is a very high mortality rate and treatment began immediately. We were never told what had caused the clots, but the medication that Julia had been taking for cancer is known to cause clots as a side effect in rare cases. Weeks followed of daily injections of blood thinners as more tests were taken for the diabetes, which turned out to be type 1. Cancer medication was changed and changed again, each causing horrible side effects which seemed almost as bad as the disease. The long, sometimes frightening, process of education, trial and error began to treat the diabetes, resulting in constant hypos as Julia's glucose levels went so low she almost passed out and went into a coma.

When circumstances like these happen you develop a level of hypervigilance which totally consumes you. The attention you give to normal work tasks or everyday activities becomes so reduced and fractured that you have to spend twice as much time as normal to complete them, or make do with the non-completion of almost everything. Relationships become a struggle to maintain, leisure non-existent. The mind becomes a place of warfare. Before Julia's illness long walks on the hills were my religion, a way to connect with the beauty and mystery of life. Afterwards they became a kind of slow torture where the landscape around me disappeared, engulfed by a torrent of rumination descending into panic attacks which took many miles to calm. One of those long walks ended at the tiny church at Llandewi Fach in freezing rain. I walked up to the altar in the half-dark of the storm. I began to search my pockets for something to leave behind. I found a little enamel brooch in the shape of a poppy and placed it on the wooden surface. I stepped away, then walked back again, picked the brooch up, took it outside and placed it beneath a fork in the roots of the yew tree.

*

I'm visiting Dore Abbey, just over the border into Herefordshire, searching for an iron wolf's head which was brought here five centuries ago. A service has just finished and a group of elderly people are standing in the shade of a tree. I retreat to the back of the building to watch honey bees swarming into a crack in a wall. Jackdaws have stuffed the spaces beneath the eaves with twigs to create their nests and they are now swooping in and out to feed their young. I walk through ruined arches, around stone pillars. When the congregation has dwindled I quietly enter the church.

I'm in a silent passageway to the north of the main chancel. On one side is a lidless tomb, long and tapering. Opposite is a carved knight, hands crossed at his chest, feet placed on the body of a fantastic animal I cannot identify. At the end of the passage is an area where fragments of corbels and bosses, broken lintels and pillars are arranged on the floor beneath stained-glass windows. Dust motes float like glitter and the stone remnants sit in little pools of colour as if spotlit on a stage. The last members of the congregation have left and the church is now empty, the quiet in the place seeming to deepen, to shuffle and settle. The light dims. Clouds must be passing over the sun but it feels as if these shiftings are emitting from the floor and walls. A spark of sunlight passes through a high window and glances on to a large corbel stone I haven't noticed. I walk over to it and see that it is a green man, with a moon-round face and huge smile, peering out of curled leaves. The puddle of light surrounding it is tinted lemon with spots of fuchsia pink making the surface of the stone almost skinlike. As I stare at the almost living thing, a young woman I hadn't noticed, and who hasn't noticed me, begins to sing beautifully, testing the acoustics of the place, a wordless tune which slowly rises in pitch. It's a long, mournful wolf howl that rises higher and higher, becoming birdsong. The walls hone it, carrying it into every corner of the building. It rings and echoes. I inhale sharply, involuntarily, then let out a slow sob. The song trails away, rings out again, fades and rises. The green man is smiling. I am in tears.

*

I spent my twenties living and working in east London and I rapidly grew to dislike its confined spaces. Privacy and solitude are as necessary to me as food and a bed. I sought out lonely places and eventually discovered the city's abandoned graveyards. Abney Park Cemetery was within walking distance of my home and it became a refuge. I'd never known a place before so seemingly forgotten.

Scrubby vegetation grew everywhere along the paths and among the graves. Stoke Newington is occasionally portrayed as an island within the city, the place where Daniel Defoe created Robinson Crusoe. The cemetery was built over a century after the publication of the book, but perhaps its founders were inspired by the idea of a wild island. It was built as a cemetery and arboretum, the only one of its kind in London, an exotic location planted with over 2,500 species. After the bankruptcy of the management company in the 1970s its sixty thousand graves were left untended.

I remember that birdsong was ever present, layered over the hum of traffic. The smell of wildflowers mixed with city fumes. Butterflies and bees swarmed around huge, ragged buddleia bushes and foxes denned beneath the headstones. I saw more foxes in a month there than I've seen in two decades in the Welsh hills. There is a derelict chapel in the centre of the graveyard, like a tiny ruined castle. Its windows and doors were voids, but the stone walls channelled the birdsong and honed it to bell clarity. There was something older than the ancient city in those grounds.

There is skill in un-tending to our spaces, in patiently leaving them to their own remaking. It's a skill that is vital now, when the damage we've done to Earth has become so urgently in need of reversal. Some of the best examples we have are to be found in old churchyards. We can enter and quietly watch the slow unfurling of the space. Perhaps we can rediscover our sense of the sacred.

*

I'm driving along a narrow Pembrokeshire lane with high hedges either side. In front of me the sun is getting low, dazzling me as I try to navigate each twist in the road. Every few hundred metres the hedges are broken by a barred gate which gives a glimpse over the fields sloping down to the sea. The lane descends and now I can see Skomer Island straight ahead, beyond a strait of dazzling water, a toothed skyline, the island silhouetted with the sun directly behind it. I turn into the campsite, pitch my tent in a hurry, then walk the few acres of common at the end of the peninsula, almost wild with neglect, a place of rock towers, Bronze Age cairns, dizzyingly high cliffs drilled deep with sea caves. The best lookout point is on a flat, lichen-graffitied boulder near to the cliff edge. From there I can see down into a horseshoe cove and over the sound to Skomer, Skokholm and distant Grassholm, a swan-white pyramid on the horizon. The sun is touching the horizon, losing its shape, beginning to crumple as if it has hit the wall of the sea. Then it slips down sending a cloud of slow-changing colours miles across the sky. Twilight descends bringing a lulled awe to the land.

Below me, a dark shape flows and twists just beneath the surface of the water, then rises; a cow seal. She hangs still, her coal eyes watching the cliffs, swims into shallow water and hauls out on to the beach. A fulmar whirrs above her, following the arc of the cliff, then flies out towards the island. Jack Sound, the narrow stretch of constantly churning water between the peninsula and Skomer Island, is calm for now, the tide only just beginning to run north. Soon it will rip and boil. A lobsterman is speeding his boat across the bay. As I follow the boat's wake with my binoculars I start to see gathering rafts of seabirds: guillemots, puffins, razorbills, thousands of them, like spills on the water. Over the island's towers and mounds there are the pterodactyl-like shapes of greater black-backed gulls, swirling in spirals.

The silhouette of the island reveals a large, half-ruined house and barn which was the home of the last family to farm the island, abandoned half a century ago after a disastrous year when they were unable to get their potato crop to market due to bad weather. Since then the island has increasingly become a hotspot for the summer migrations of pelagic birds. It is the world's primary breeding place for Manx shearwaters, three-quarters of a million of them, which nest in burrows dug into the old fields. The birds are silent in the day, hiding from predating gulls. At night, the partners who have been feeding at sea come home in a great flock, calling to their mates in spooky ululations, scudding into their burrows to feed chicks. I spent a night on the island sitting in darkness long past midnight waiting for them to come, listening to the beckoning calls of the gulls. They didn't arrive. That night it was too clear, too moonlit, too dangerous to return. But my vigil was rewarded at dawn when short-eared owls swooped low and silent over my head, hunting in zigzags.

Skomer was inhabited by humans for millennia. It contains some of the most pristine archaeological sites in the UK, a landscape of hill forts, cairns, tumuli, standing stones and ancient field systems. Beyond its cliffs there are strangely configured sea stacks and islets, like roughly formed chapels and lone steeples.

Though little research has been undertaken, the density of its monuments suggest a sacred landscape, orientated almost perfectly east to west. Even the sword-like shape of the island looks like a ritual object given to the sea. In the autumn, when the summer migrants have returned to the deep ocean, a religious quiet descends on the place when the sea is calm and an Old Testament fury when storms come in. It is a place of peace, and terror. I don't know of anywhere more beautiful. My family have been visiting for years, going in all weathers. We've frozen on the cliffs in spring, watching for returning puffins, and sat among a sea of bluebells in early summer while porpoises breached below us. We've crossed Jack Sound while a storm was building, the little boat lurching wildly, almost throwing us overboard, and we've waited long past midnight to watch the shearwaters coming back to their nests. It's the most sacred place I know, the place I go to when I need reassurance that we can still live symbiotically with the wild, that this ancient land filled with ghosts can transform quickly into a landscape of life. The volunteers and wardens who look after the island have a clear reverence for the place, its myriad species and deep history. This twilight we're inhabiting now, this draining down of life, is a kind of oppression for people who have a deep connection to wild places. We need time on our little islands. Inhabiting them, even for a brief period, is a form of nourishment. It's in these places that we can heal before returning to the fight.

*

Overlooking the little church at Llandewi Fach, at sixteen hundred feet, the highest point on the hill, there is another church of sorts. It is walled with stone, but the roof is a canopy of trees. It was built a century ago and people have come here since on short pilgrimages, walking west across the common and climbing the long slope to the gated gap in the wall. They come here on Christmas morning to light a fire and drink a toast. For Queen Elizabeth II's golden jubilee they built two rows of flaming beacons as a walkway to the summit that burned from dusk to dawn. It is a landmark that can be seen from every summit for miles, ancient-looking, like a Stone Age monument. Buried within it, and almost completely erased, is a real tomb, just a spoon-shaped indent in the ground now, with only a few loose stones revealing a fragment of its original structure. Out of it protrude the leaning trunks of trees, immature and wind-twisted. My kids climbed them when they were little and we sheltered underneath them when we were caught in hail, or snowstorms. Other people have left memorial stones here, or have scattered the ashes of loved ones. It is a place of secular worship.

It is also favoured by the wild inhabitants of the hill. Golden plovers roost just outside all winter, perfectly camouflaged against the bracken stubble. Red kites and buzzards swing over the trees and wheatears perch on the walls. Once I saw a raven sparring with a peregrine falcon here, the corvid playing a game, flipping upside down and twisting in the air while the raptor, crazed with bloodlust, dived and swooped to try to seize it in its talons. It failed over and over again. In the end the falcon gave up and flew off while the raven watched its enemy retreat, throwing insults as it went. The trees are Corsican pines, ill-fitted to the terrain. Their canopies have spread sideways, rather than upwards, and intertwined like thatch. Beneath them, at any time between sun up and sun down, it is dusk. The quality of sound changes as you enter the trees, as in a chapel. But instead of the deadening, the shutting out of the world, beneath the trees you can hear more clearly. Sound is channelled by the always-present wind and tuned to a new pitch.

I walk to this place at least three times a week, crossing the sheep-bitten common. From as early as February there are skylarks in the air and I pass beneath flare after flare of their tremolo songs. Sometimes I don't notice. My dog trots ahead of me, examining the minutiae of the ground, tracing last night's stories of fox and hare. The climb leaves me out of breath, heart thumping, sweat on my skin. But, in a whirl of thought, I simply walk around the walls and keep walking, back down the hill, past the roosting plovers, beneath the red kites and buzzards, the merlins, wheatears, redstarts and yellowhammers, noticing none of them. These are the days of half-light. On occasional walks the cacophony inside me is stilled early by a sight or sound which stops me in my tracks: wind-creased light on the pool, sun rays angling from clouds, swans crossing the hill. The rumination disappears and I become aware, the closest I can get to pure awareness, for an instant. Afterwards my thoughts are quieter, my attention directed outwards. I climb the hill, enter through the gate and sit for a while on the stone bench that arcs out from the pines, looking across the valley. I watch the clouds materialising, dematerialising. I step into the vault beneath the trees.

*

There is a man climbing a steep hill at sunset. He is panting as he rushes to get to the summit before the sun dips below the horizon, an African, plummeting sun. The ground is dry and red dust kicks up with each step. This is not the man's native soil. He is a long way from home. When he arrived here he was a young anthropologist with a research grant to last a year. He would be studying a tribe of hunter-gatherers who had never been studied before, trying to understand the origins of human culture. On his return home after that first year he missed the place so badly that he immediately approached the institution for more funding and within weeks he was back in Africa. This process continued for two decades.

Finally the research is complete and he needs to go home to write the book that will be the culmination of the project. He has packed his bags, said goodbye to his friends of twenty years and now wants to take one last look at the landscape before he heads to the airport. He reaches the summit of the hill and looks down across a forest which trills with the sounds of its wild inhabitants.

The sun is getting low, growing as its shape is refracted through the air. It bulges and ripples as if pushed by the wind which now starts to cool his face and caress his nostrils. He takes a deep breath. A dark shape enters the tail of his eye, moving across the slope below him. He sees a long-limbed monkey crossing the path. It is carrying what looks like a melon in its arms. It stops and turns to the sun. The monkey stands up on its back legs, lifts the melon high above its head, holding it in both paws, and stays in that position while the sun melts into the jungle. The anthropologist is incredulous. He has never witnessed this before, has never heard of anything like it from his bushmen companions, or the scientists he communicates with. He turns and walks down the hill knowing that everything he has studied for twenty years has been worthless. He goes back to his cases filled with notes and destroys them all.

The indigenous activist and Nobel Peace Prize nominee Tiokasin Ghosthorse related this apparently true story when speaking to students at Yale University. He felt that the people he was addressing were possessed by the desire to take knowledge from other cultures in order to gain ascendancy in their own lives and careers. The anthropologist in the story learned humility in the face of mystery.

A sense of the sacred may not be unique to humans. The primatologist Jane Goodall witnessed chimpanzee behaviour at the edges of a high waterfall in Gombe National Park. She described how the chimps approached the falls very differently to other features in the landscape and the way their whole demeanour changed. They slowed down and began to sway as they neared the water, then lifted rocks and threw them out into the stream, like offerings. They climbed vines and swung across the falls, deliberately passing through the spray, then sat at the foot staring at the water tumbling towards and rushing past them, as if lost in contemplation. This behaviour has been recorded on video and widely viewed. Goodall believes it to be a display ritual, an act of reverence by the chimps, and perhaps a sign of the origins of spirituality in primates which could have happened long before the human species evolved.

*

Follow the stream that runs past the whipping tree, trickles around the graveyard, then crosses beneath the lane and flows down the fold in the land that runs from the mountain, cutting deeper as it goes. It heads into the dusk of wooded gorges, stepping down fault after fault in bedrock four hundred million years old, freckled with the fossils of sea creatures. Deep in one of these gorges the stream forks and drops vertically twenty metres into a wide pool, a high waterfall almost identical to the one the chimps go to in Gombe. According to local history this is another place we used for our punishments. It is called Pwll-y-Wrach, the witches' pool.

The pool is surrounded by an amphitheatre of rock overhung with trees, a forbidding place, a place to stand and stare down into the water while the torrent consumes its victim. Or so the story suggests. But the idea that this place was used to persecute witches is certainly false. There were few cases of witch persecution in Wales and there is plenty of evidence to suggest that they were tolerated here much more than in the rest of the UK. The pool itself is less than a metre deep, almost circular and, with the curved rock surrounding it, it resembles a cauldron. The association with witches is surely a reference to the shape of the place.

The surrounding wood has been left unmanaged for a while. The paths have become overgrown, crowded in by branches of holly and hazel, nettle spears, bramble whips. It is late afternoon on a bright day, but the falls are in half-light, with only a feathered gap high above letting in the sky. The deep green of ash and hazel leaves smother the rest. The stream bed and the rocks are the colours of sunset, the sandstone ochre red.

We came here frequently when our boys were small. They paddled in the pool, then screeched as they got soaked beneath the falls, battered by the icy water. They clawed and squeezed clods from the earth in their little fists, threw them into the pool and watched as they dissolved in a cloud of red. In places where algae coated the stream bed they lay down and let the water carry them, slippery as fish, taking part in the flow of the place. I come here now to sit silently and watch, to give trees and water my attention. Dippers arrive frequently, clad in black and white, their movements stilted and twitchy, like shy vicars. A yellow wagtail perches on the edge of the pool, caught in a glint of sunlight which bounces on the water. It flits away into the wood, then returns, as if it's forgotten to do something. One tail of the waterfall catches the light, white as a swan's feather, while the other is shaded blue-green.

There are people on this planet, members of cultures who still view the land as a home for the gods, who would come here to worship. They would instantly recognise the deep life of the place. They would sing as they scattered flowers on the pool, watching them drift out of sight downstream, into the hands of the water and tree spirits. They would look up to the sky, at the protecting arms of the oaks, and make an arc with their hands to mark the passing of the light. They would blow a handful of dust into the air so they could see the breathing of the falls. Then they would bow, devout as the dipper.

THE LION, THE WOLF AND THE CURLEW

I'd like to be out on the African savannah, listening to the night sounds coming from every direction, an interspecies conversation, dusk to dawn, the landscape singing with life. But instead I'm waiting for a distant owl call coming from a bone tree, the music of this place. It is twilight on a day at year's end. I'm sitting in silence, watching the sky go dark through the window, thin clouds moving south, colours grey to violet. Beyond the garden hedge is a field and in its top corner is the darker-than-black skeleton of an oak. There are seven big oaks between my house and the pine plantation up on the hill. Some are ancient. One, in the past year, has become diseased and its branches, once fanned with an ever more delicate tracery of twigs, are now blunt antlers. At twilight it looks part animal.

Only minutes ago I could see the edge of the garden, which is now a black, bristling wall. Two chaffinches were on the bird feeder, dipping their heads politely to pick seeds. Then a shadow blurred across the window, twisted, changed direction and skidded into the feeder. There was a short, piercing shriek and one of the finches was gone. The blur landed on the grass and became a sparrowhawk. It spooked and flew off towards the oak tree, which is now a smudge against a turquoise-to-lead sky. The lights in the room have appeared on the surface of the window, floating, their coiled filaments luminescent. Superimposed over them is the faint image of a Georgia O'Keeffe painting. Minutes pass and the oak disappears into the almost indigo clouds. The reflected room fades in.

I'm struggling to read an account of an African twilight which I last read more than a quarter of a century ago, one of the stories which eventually led me there. It is dusk and two hunters are walking through elephant grass. They have glimpsed a rhino heading into forest cover less than a mile ahead, but now they have heard the cough of a lion. They don't know how close it is and whether it can see them. The cover is too deep, too dangerous, they must retreat back to the safety of camp. I find this second reading of *Green Hills of Africa* hard going. The prose is still beautiful, but Hemingway's values are repulsive, the way he finds beauty in decapitated heads, his comic sense of pain and death. In the century since his trip to Tanzania, eastern black rhinos, which appeared to him almost as regularly as cattle, have been decimated. There are less than eighty left. Most have been shot, initially by trophy hunters, more recently by poachers. In Hemingway's dusk scene I see the deeper shadows of extinction, creeping in with a slow-acting, lethal poison.

The reflections of the lights are brighter against the window, the black wires that suspend them clearly visible. The outside world has disappeared. The only natural forms I can see are the painted poppies created by O'Keeffe around the time Hemingway made his trophy-hunting trip. The window is ajar, I leave it open so I can listen for owls. But tonight there is nothing to hear.

*

In East Africa the sky has a presence both inspiring in its vastness and ominous in its transformations. The indigo dark that now gathers on the horizon moves in fast and creaturely. We are sitting beside a fire under a sky that is rapidly draining of light. A circle of trees surrounds us, umbrellas of darkness against a cloudless backdrop. We've been out all day in a battered van in search of the big five: buffalo, elephant, lion, leopard, rhino. We found four. The highlight has been getting too close to a scar-faced lioness camouflaged in the shade of a tree. Around it were zebras and antelopes, unconcerned by the lion's presence as it lay panting and yawning, its belly so full it was almost immobile. Later we found the corpse of a buffalo, its legs splayed, bones protruding, and the rest of the pride fast asleep on a nearby rock, a pile of bloated kittens. We'd seen cheetahs, wildebeest in huge numbers, a small herd of elephants, several species of antelope, and many fabulously coloured birds I will never know the names of. In the heat everything moved in slow motion, the animals at leisure as if taking an interlude in their lives, rather than attending to life itself. Tribesmen sat beneath trees, or leaned on spears, idle sentinels watching their bony cattle. It was like a film that required editing, under-paced, loosely scripted, awaiting an action scene.

The light is fading now and with it cool pillows of air are descending to the baked ground carrying scents that I have never smelled before. People talk and drink by the fire, a little about what they witnessed out on the plain, but mostly of the usual things, the routines and obsessions carried here from home. I say nothing. I'm trying to listen to the sounds beyond the pool of firelight. Gradually the others go to bed and I'm left alone by the fire, which has just been stoked by a Masai youth whose job it is to keep watch. He sits on a handmade wooden stool, disinterested, at home. I hear something moving not too far away, then a pause, and then more sounds, like the drumming of hooves. A shriek, a fluttering. Something is being shaken to death. I'm staring into the shadows, seeing nothing, not knowing what I should expect to see. I turn to the boy, who is also listening, but he seems unconcerned. I retreat to my tent, spend the whole night concentrating hard on the soundscape beyond the thin, fabric walls, little scribbles and rushes of noise made by the wind. At around 3 a.m. I hear the low, moaning roar of a lion and I sit up. I edge to the front of the tent, stare out. The fire is still burning, the boy still tending it. My heart is pounding. My skin is wet. I feel light-headed, unable to fully catch my breath. I've heard the roar of a wild lion, felt it reverberating through me, like a memory.

Our recall can be multigenerational. The sound of the lion's roar, carried by the stillness of an African night, woke something inside me long forgotten. I heard it the way an animal hears, with all my two hundred bones reverberating. Though I recognised the sound from TV programmes and films, there was an older memory, species deep. For the first time since I was a child, maybe the first time ever, I was listening.

The visceral sense that the world breathes and feeds needs to be reawakened in our lives. Out in the wild, modern civilisation is only surface deep. The rest, our whole animal evolution, is as bottomless as the memory of the earth. J.R.R. Tolkien once described memory as being like a photographic plate or film. Repeated shots of the same scene create an over-exposure resulting in a faint image or even a blank. For the years preceding my journey to Africa I had been doing the same job, in the same place, my life orbiting a small circle, following the same routes. The streets I walked down had become ghosted out, my senses numbed. But, in an instant, I had become vulnerable, open to the world and all its wounds. I remembered my place.

*

In 1937, workmen digging in the old moat of the Tower of London discovered two perfectly preserved lion skulls. Scientists carbon-dated the skulls and estimated that one lion had lived in the fifteenth century, the other in the thirteenth. Lions were given as gifts by foreign dignitaries to the kings of England and were kept in the Tower of London, where they were displayed at the gates as symbols of strength and sovereignty. The two skulls were identified as Barbary lions, a species that once inhabited the whole of Africa north of the Sahara. An examination of one of the skulls revealed a bony protrusion where the spinal cord enters the brain, a sign of sickness, most probably caused by malnutrition. Pressure on the spinal cord from this piece of bone would have caused partial or total paralysis and blindness. The lions of England, guardians of the crown, would have been sorry specimens.

The custom of giving Barbary lions as gifts to heads of state continued in Morocco well into the twentieth century. The sultan's menagerie contained more than twenty, kept at his palace in Rabat, until the 1950s when he was forced into exile. Afterwards the lions were separated and transferred to zoos, where many of them were cross-bred with lions from Asia. It is not known if there is a single Barbary lion left on Earth. Years of being captured for zoos or hunted for sport, the decimation of their wild prey and the increase in human population led to their range shrinking dramatically until they were confined to remote areas of the Atlas Mountains. They were declared extinct in the wild in 1922. But sightings of lions continued to be reported by remote mountain communities. These sightings were always of a single lion and none were proven. It was as if the ghosts of the species were being reported, the memory of them still present in the places they once roamed. The sightings continued for decades until, in the 1960s, they ceased. Today a search is ongoing for a living, genetically distinct Barbary lion in the remaining captive populations. None have yet been found.

The only lion species to inhabit the British Isles was the cave lion, which went extinct in Europe approximately ten thousand years ago. Fossil remains are only occasionally found in the UK and we know very little about them except that they utilised caves as shelters in a similar way to humans. There is evidence from Cantabria in Spain that cave lions were hunted for their skins and this may have been a contributing factor to their extinction, but the archaeology is too slight to draw any firm conclusions. They ranged across most of the Holarctic but disappeared swiftly over a period of a few thousand years. In 2017, the body of a cave lion cub was found in permafrost in the Russian republic of Yakutia. The cub was photographed with its head still resting on its paws, a plump kitten, not much bigger than a domestic cat, with tan coat and long whiskers. It was almost fifty thousand years old. It is the best sample ever discovered of cave lion remains and was sent to universities, where its DNA was extracted and archived. Two years earlier, after flooding on the Uyandina River caused permafrost to crack and slip, an ice lens was found by scientists searching for mammoth remains. Inside were the bodies of two cave lion cubs. Though not as well preserved as the later discovery, they still had their milk teeth, fur and whiskers. They were dated at forty thousand years old. All three cubs are now the subject of speculation about the possibility of de-extinction. After centuries of capturing lions to be caged and chained for display, after decimating wild populations everywhere in their natural range, we are now contemplating bringing back a subspecies that no human has encountered for ten millennia.

There are many companies worldwide developing techniques for species de-extinction, but perhaps the most eye-catching project is being carried out by the US-based company Colossal, who propose to bring back the woolly mammoth. One of Colossal's stated aims, on the slick website they've created to market the project, is to restore a huge area of the subarctic to conditions similar to those when mammoths were extant. The far north at that time was made up of savannah, vegetation consisting mainly of grasses. Today these areas are home to boggy forests colonised by mosses, radically different to the places the mammoths inhabited and helped to maintain. The hypothesis is that by recreating the species, using existing African elephants as surrogates, the mammoths' feeding and migratory patterns will return the land to savannah, a more resilient ecosystem. This could ultimately ameliorate climate change, savannah being more efficient at storing carbon. The now rapidly thawing permafrost could refreeze. The company states that they would be creating a mammoth-like animal, and not an exact copy of the original species. In effect they will be originating a new species. To date they have raised seventy-five million dollars in funds, some of the investors including well-known celebrities and futurist billionaires. They estimate that the first mammoth will be born in 2027.

To successfully create enough individuals to form herds large enough to change an ecosystem that currently covers most of Siberia, Alaska, the Northwest Territories and the Yukon, an area of more than twenty million square miles, is an immense task which could only be proposed by members of a society completely out of touch with the ecosystems they believe they can repair. Creating even a single woolly mammoth is fraught with difficulties. A recent research project examined the possibility of reproducing the genome of the Christmas Island rat, a species that went extinct in the early twentieth century. When the gene sequence was mapped the scientists found that approximately 4 per cent of the genome could not be recovered, even though the reference was of very high quality. Genetic information degrades and slowly disappears over time, even over the relatively short period of a century. They concluded that it would be impossible to recover this 4 per cent of genetic information in any species intended for de-extinction. Additionally, they found that the missing genetic information in the test case affected the rat's olfactory sense and its immune system, which would be vital for the species' survival if it were to be reintroduced to its original habitat.

A study looking at the conditions and events that led to the extinction of the woolly mammoth which had been ongoing for ten years was recently completed. Its aim was to establish whether human activity was a factor, a theory that has been proposed many times. Woolly mammoths were extant in the Holarctic for more than five million years, surviving multiple ice ages before humans began to colonise their environment. The project used DNA shotgun sequencing taken from soil samples over an extensive period and eventually sequenced the DNA of more than fifteen hundred plants as part of the research. This data gave the scientists an in-depth view of the environment which the mammoths inhabited and led them to the conclusion that the extinction had been caused by sudden climate warming which led to much higher levels of rainfall, drowning the savannah and creating lakes and boggy forests. These areas are now transforming again at a pace far more rapid and unpredictable than the warming experienced by the mammoths, trees encroaching northwards into tundra areas creating new biomes as the ice melts.

*

I had a childhood friend who could draw perfectly from memory. He didn't need paper, brushes or pencils. He could use sticks, nails, flakes of stone, lumps of coal. Everywhere he went he left behind an image. Once, in a field of snow, I watched him as he hopped backwards in a long curve almost half the length of the field, his left foot dragging on the ground. He stopped, walked lightly back to the centre of the arc and started again. The drag marks became a bear fifty metres long. Whenever he drew he seemed to step out of himself, to become almost translucent against the image he was creating. Later in life I discovered the images in the caves of Chauvet, Lascaux and Altamira and I thought of his work.

The panel of the lions, deep inside the labyrinth at Chauvet, depicts a hunt. On the right of the composition are the shapes of woolly rhinoceroses, aurochs, mammoths and bison. Behind them are the figures of a pride of lions, depicted mostly by their heads and necks, their torsos and legs blending into other outlines and contours running along the surface of the rock. An auroch looks out into the open space of the cave. Two lions are nose to nose. The other animals face left as if running in the same direction, the herd pursued, the pride in pursuit. The lions are rendered differently, some very realistically, others less so. There are lines drawn over older lines, repeated mark-making, one artist following the shapes another made years earlier. The art in the cave was an act of communal memory, intersecting and overlapping, crafted by earlier generations, perhaps centuries, or even millennia, apart. The lions were brought back to life through art, their shapes viewed in the flickering twilight created by hearths and torches, casting shadowy undulations along the walls, animating everything. It is likely that the caves were places of communal ritual. The dark spaces were not only filled with memorised shapes, but also the echoing sounds of the animals, mimicked by the hunter-gatherers, the roar and bellow, scream and thunder of pursuit. It is strange to us, viewing the images from a thirty-millennia distance, that among the perfectly rendered wild forms painted and engraved on the rock, there are only very sporadic attempts to depict humans. Those that are present lack the animation and fluidity of the animals. It's as if the artists were unable to remember their own shapes.

*

When I was a boy I had a beautifully illustrated encyclopedia of animals which I spent a lot of time with, thumbing through page after page to stare at ocelots, red pandas, blue whales, pit vipers, tropical birds and huge pearlescent insects. It's the only book I've ever owned which I could call a companion. I would hold it and run my fingers along the edges, then allow the book to fall open to see which animal wanted to appear. One had a full-page illustration of a grey wolf sitting on its haunches, staring out with eyes that wouldn't let me go. The illustration was so real I was convinced that the wolf was about to spring out of the book into my tiny bedroom. The possibility terrified me. I started to avoid it, creasing the page corner so I wouldn't accidentally open it. Later, to make sure it could never be opened again, I sealed it shut with tape (I couldn't tear the page out, books are too important to me). There were other pictures in the book, just as convincing and well executed, of hammerhead sharks, Siberian tigers, hyenas and boa constrictors, but none of these spooked me in the same way as the wolf. They were pictures whereas the wolf was a presence, a possibility. A memory.

Around the time that I sealed the wolf into the pages of my encyclopedia I visited the grave of Gelert in North Wales. An engraved stone told the story of how a prince of Gwynedd went out hunting with his hounds, but forgot to take his favourite dog, Gelert, with him. When the prince returned he went to visit his infant son in his nursery. The child's cot was upside down and the walls and floor of the room were spattered with blood. Gelert ran into the room to greet his master. The hound's jaws and fur were bloody. The prince, thinking that the hound had killed his baby, drew his sword and thrust it into the dog. As he stood over Gelert's body he heard the cries of his son and moved the upturned cot to see that the baby was lying on the floor unharmed. Next to the boy was the body of a wolf. The little mound, headstone and plaque for Gelert were created by a local hotel owner in the late eighteenth century to encourage tourism. There was no Gelert or prince, just a story to stir our memories and fears. For me, the wolves were still out there, roaming the mountains of Wales.

The ruins of the old abbey are visible in the churchyard. Tumbled and fractured walls lean out towards apple trees in the neglected orchard. The grass is knee high, nettles even higher. I've been exploring the place for hours, trying to find the relic I've read about. The stories say that it was fixed to one of the doors, but I've checked them all, inside and out, and I've found nothing. It may have been taken elsewhere, stolen or lost. It may never have existed. Stories twist and turn like memories. They sometimes shift places or bubble up out of nowhere. This area was once known as Archenfield, a wild and lawless place spanning the land between the River Wye and the ramparts of the Black Mountains. It was somewhere in the twilit gloom of the forest that once surrounded the abbey where the last wolf in England was exterminated by the hunter Peter Corbett, sent on an eight-year campaign to bring about the extinction of the species by King Edward I. The king commissioned Corbett to hunt all the lands from Staffordshire to Gloucestershire. To commemorate the success of the mission a wolf's head was forged by a blacksmith and mounted on one of the church doors at Dore Abbey. After the campaign there were few accounts of wolf sightings and it is likely that the species went extinct in England at that time. Somewhere in the church grounds the wolf's head may still exist, a memorial to extinction and a symbol of human triumph that is, to me, one of mourning.

There is another book which has been important in my life, one I've come back to again and again, particularly in recent years. *Among Wolves* is a collection of writings by biologist Gordon Haber, who devoted much of his life to studying wolves in Denali National Park, Alaska, and to protecting the species. Haber's work was extraordinarily detailed. He monitored wolf packs constantly, observing their lives in all situations, whether they were hunting, preparing for a hunt, feeding or sleeping. He researched the conditions when wolves were most likely to howl, their denning habits and how they raised pups and taught juveniles to cross terrain and hunt large prey. At the same time he fought the many groups and individuals that sought to exterminate wolves in the area. In the book are many of the photographs he took of packs. One series of pictures stands out and I refer back to them constantly. It shows a group of six wolves crossing a fast-moving river with a steep cutback on one side. The group consisted of two adult females, a yearling and three pups. The adult females led the group across the water and continued on their route but the three pups were frightened to cross. The yearling watched over them from the opposite side of the river, encouraging them to cross by crouching down and flicking the water with her paws in an act of pretend play. The pups still would not cross. When one of them decided to brave it the yearling went back and walked with it through the river, trying to keep it moving, but the pup spooked and retreated. The situation continued until another pup made the attempt. This time the yearling crossed and stood downstream of the pup, bracing it against the current. When it reached the other side the yearling leaned into the water to help it climb the steep bank. The other two pups followed. Haber theorised that these cooperative skills, demonstrated in all wolf activities, amounted to a culture and fought hard to protect the species on that basis. He died while monitoring wolves from a plane. Two hikers were crossing a mountain ridge nearby when it happened. They reported that they could hear the plane circling in the distance. The engine noise went dead and a brief silence followed. Then they heard, coming from all directions, the sounds of wolves howling, a final proof of Haber's theory.

I don't like to imagine the moment when the huntsman came across the ragged animal, caught in a trap and already near to death. He would have taken his blade, gone to its side and slid a stripe across its throat to empty the last blood from a species that had inhabited these islands for twelve thousand years. Wolves had been persecuted in England for centuries before Corbett's campaign. Thirty thousand wolf skins had already been paid by the Welsh as tribute to English kings by the time the Normans invaded and there were no recorded wolf sightings in Wales after the twelfth century. Our last big carnivore was already a ghost presence in the English landscape by the thirteenth century and Corbett may not have been responsible for their extinction. The most likely cause was the genetic weakness of a minuscule and bedraggled population, unable to maintain a territory, forced to move continually to survive until there were only one or two packs left, too distant from each other to breed, already functionally extinct. It is possible that no human witnessed the death of the last wolf in these lands.

*

It took thirty years for the wolf, sealed between the pages of my encyclopedia, to escape. We were travelling on a dirt road through a Canadian forest that stretched for miles. Either side were rows and rows of tree trunks striated with pale diagonals where the sun needled through the canopy. In the distance we could occasionally glimpse the white peak of a mountain, the wall of a glacier. We had been told of a pool as blue as topaz, glittering with silver sediment, icebergs stranded like giant toadstools on its edge. The forest was motionless, as if nothing existed except for the trees, much like the pine plantations back in Wales. And then the wolf stepped out. Or leaped out, or flowed out. It turned and sat down, right in front of us. It was identical to the one in the encyclopedia, blue-grey coat, cream undersides, ears erect, the pallor of its green eyes enhanced by the surrounding black markings. It stared straight at us, still as an image on a page. Wolves are wired to flee from humans, but this one was totally unconcerned. I spoke to experts about the encounter and most didn't believe me. A few theorised that the animal must have been sick or dying, that it either couldn't see us

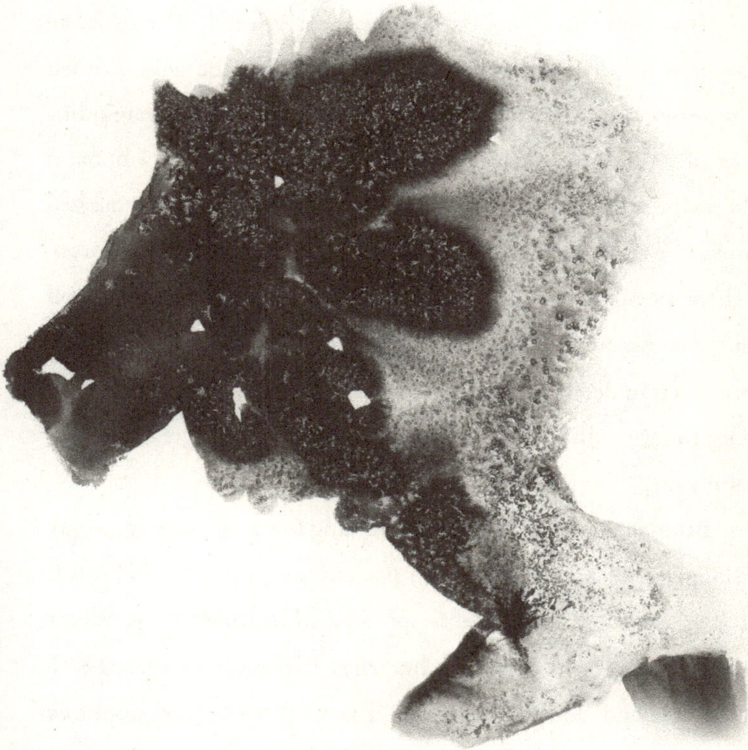

or that it was too exhausted to care. That was not the case. When the wolf finally went on its way it turned and leaped in one bound across the track and ran flat out up the steep slope.

That experience was one of the most visceral of my life, an interspecies close encounter, a one-to-one with the wild. I've felt ever since that the wolf was questioning me somehow, reminding me of an old friendship. In our distant past wolves and humans hunted the same prey. We inhabited their dens and they inhabited ours. We tamed them eight thousand years before we tamed horses. There are many threads running through our lives made from wolf fur. The knowledge that they are still out there, running through the twilit understorey of distant forests, makes me happy. I've been face to face with a wild wolf and it was one of the great honours of my life.

After that encounter the surrounding forest became animated. The place wasn't like the tamed plantations back in Wales, it was full of wildlife. Herds of elks appeared in clearings. Huge ravens shouted slurs at us from high branches. Red squirrels chased each other up and down tree trunks. The work of beavers appeared in boggy ponds and little streams. We saw rivers teeming with salmon, mountain goats high up on crags, circled by bald eagles. On a hike up a tree-lined gorge we passed within a few metres of a moose which seemed to acknowledge us quietly and then went back to its grazing.

*

Years ago my father was walking home from work along a path that crossed through an area of waste ground. Those places were common all over the city, areas where shafts and quarries had been filled in and left. They were ruined places with sour, oil-coated pools and streams, where nothing grew, memorials to a time when Stoke had been one of the smoking bonfires of the industrial revolution. It was a late-autumn dusk. A man was coming up the path dressed in the old style of suit, waistcoat and cap. As they passed each other the man touched his cap, nodded and said good evening. My father absent-mindedly walked past without a greeting, then turned back to speak. The man had disappeared. There was nowhere he could have gone. He was convinced he'd seen a ghost.

Some places are replete with memories. So many lives have passed through them that they hold on to their traces and echoes. Perhaps memories walk, visible to some at twilight, their shapes indistinct, *entre chien et loup* – between dog and wolf. In densely historied places we remain familiar with the things that have passed away, able to recall them somehow, like the lions of the Atlas Mountains, extinct for decades and yet still seen by the people who had crossed paths with them for millennia. They fade away gradually, over centuries, first their shapes, and then, at last, their cries.

Towards the end of my father's decline from Parkinson's disease I was researching the biodiversity crisis, particularly the conditions which were pushing species towards extinction locally. I was now witnessing these first-hand and was starting to feel hopeless, about the possibilities of ameliorating the problems, and about the future of my two boys. The developing crisis became, for me, not only external, but internal. A mild depression started deepening. Long walks on the hill helped little. I would get lost in swirling thoughts, letting them drift inside me like squalls. I would walk further and faster, until my hips ached with the effort of climbing and descending slopes. Most days I would notice little of my surroundings. I was studying curlews at the time, they had become a symbol of the crisis for me. The local population had fallen precipitously and were on the brink. The Eurasian curlew is a bird with a huge range and internationally, though vulnerable due to slowly declining numbers, it is not threatened. But in Wales, where their upland habitat has been decimated, the species will go extinct soon. For several years, at the beginning and end of every breeding season, I watched the skies for their arrival and departure, hoping that their numbers had increased. And every year they shrank, until there were only two or three pairs left. It felt to me as if the fragility of their relationship with the place had become viscerally connected to my own ability to hold on as I began to be buffeted by losses. I went to meeting after meeting with conservationists proposing projects to reverse their decline. I came away from all of those meetings feeling that there was little chance of success. There were obvious divisions of opinion about how the projects would work, and who would benefit, which always seemed to be the real focus of attention. In the end, several years of work and millions of pounds spent resulted in no increase in curlew numbers on the local hills.

Parkinson's disease is an illness which strips away physical and mental capacities tectonically. There are periods when the decline is so gradual it is imperceptible, followed by sudden shocks and descents. At the beginning of my father's illness I only noticed that his right hand shook a little, that when he walked his steps were a little shorter. After a few years, the walk suddenly became a shuffle, and a slur in his speech appeared. Later he began to move his head when he spoke, pushing his chin up and to one side as if the words were heavy and he had to haul them out. Then he started to lose his balance and walking became a fraught activity. A stick was necessary, then a walking frame and a scooter. A stairlift was installed, a hoist to lift him into bed. In the weeks before he died he lay in a metal cot in the living room, unable to move, speak or even swallow.

Place cells are found in the hippocampus. These neurons fire in patterns known as place fields, which respond to locations and enable humans and animals to navigate. On entering a location a unique pattern will fire within the fields creating a non-topographical map which then fires again when that place is remembered. The patterns are hexagonal. It was recently discovered that place cells also have a crucial function in the recall of memories. The process operates in the same way, utilising hexagonal grids. Our memories are literally bonded to a place and stored as navigable maps inside us. It is one of the oldest evolutionary functions of the brain.

The ability to navigate is one of the first things that disappear with the onset of neuro-degenerative diseases like dementia, years before other cognitive functions are compromised. Though

Parkinson's disease mainly affects a person's muscles it can also bring on a form of dementia. This was the case for Dad. His recall shrank as the illness progressed, like a reservoir drying out. The landscape of his life was the sprawling city, which he knew intimately, remembering where old houses, factories, playing fields, railways, pits and quarries had been before they were built on. Beyond the city were the green spaces he loved, the moors, rolling pastures and woodlands of Staffordshire and the Peak District. This extended place memory, learned by his feet over eight decades, shrank to the size of a small, twilit room, and the view through a window, which he recognised less and less.

A body is also a place. The landscape of my dad's body was eroded, bitten away by the disease. The last few times I visited him in hospital I would walk up and down the ward unable to find him. Then I would suddenly recognise him. I would walk to his bed, touch his fragile hands. He would wake and stare fiercely through me. Then he'd pass beyond that layer that lies between sleep and waking, and manage to whisper – hello kid. In the final weeks of his life I watched him disappear from view. I never knew if what I was saying to him to try to ease his suffering was heard, or even if he suffered at all. I still don't know what I did right, only the things I did wrong, the things I didn't say, the invasive medical procedures I shouldn't have allowed, the rituals I didn't know that could have helped.

*

All day squalls have been scudding along the valley, rain battering down then clearing to a glaring sky filled with rainbows. The coronavirus lockdown has begun in the UK. For the first time in years the graziers have moved all their sheep off the common, perhaps worried that the virus can be spread to, or via, their animals. The hill is empty. It is normal to experience quiet here, but usually the peace is punctuated by the sounds of tractors and sheep, or planes overhead. Today there are no vapour trails in the sky and even the crows are observing silence. At this time of year the hill is bone bare, bitten back by hard winter weather, the bracken that covers most of the ground in summer still dormant. To the west the volcano-shaped peaks of the Brecon Beacons glow green in a pool of sunlight while the ridges of the Black Mountains are smoke dark with rain. I head for the pool, the best place on the hill to see birds, though for the past few weeks it has been unusually empty of the passage migrants which often rest and feed here. No sign yet of the teal, tufted ducks, Canada geese and swans. For several years the curlews that come to breed in this area have frequented the fields which border the pool. I haven't seen them this year and I'm not sure if they've arrived yet. A dense plantation of pine trees blocks the view to the big, boggy field they prefer. They're elusive, slow moving, well camouflaged, only declaring themselves with their tapering calls. Like a wolf howl, it's a cry that shivers your bones.

Curlews have long been associated with loss, their calls meant to predict a death in the house if they flew over at dusk. These cries are ominous, augural. In ancient Rome an augur was called upon to interpret the future from certain signs in the land or weather, but mainly from the behaviour of birds. The word augur in Latin means 'of what birds speak'. The sense of the importance of bird speech reached back to a time when gods did not take human form and inhabit citadels in the sky, but instead dwelled in the lands that surrounded us. Birds were our sixth sense.

*

There was a day, after Dad died, when a whirlwind overtook me. I walked for hours on the hill, taking tracks that crossed, recrossed and turned back on themselves, going in circles and figures of eight, going anywhere just to keep moving. Finally I came to a broken cairn at the top of a rise with a stone in its centre, shaped like a stool. I sat down and began to vocalise everything that had happened and how I felt, an emotional cry to the clouds, the wind, the earth. It only lasted a few minutes before I became acutely self-conscious and fell silent. I stared out at the landscape, at the pool glittering below. There was a single high-pitched note as a curlew rose up from a patch of bracken nearby, headed out towards the pool, then curved back to fly low over my head. As it reached me it let out its billowing call, which hung in the air. Perhaps it had heard me. Perhaps it was replying with its own sorrow. It was the time of year when it should have been raising young and it was alone, its nest having failed again.

After that encounter I began to feel that the hill was listening. I would come up to the cairn regularly to whisper to the place. I began to pick up stones and take them home with me. I'd paint or chalk words on to them, little poems for the place, then take them back to put into hollows, or beneath broken trees, or next to springs, songs left for a place that was also in mourning. One day I put a stone into a split in the trunk of a fallen thorn tree. When I came back a few weeks later I noticed scratch marks on its edge. Later words started to disappear from the poem, as if picked away by someone intent on correcting my work. Over time most of the letters were erased leaving a long, broken, undecipherable word, a cry in a language only known to birds.

The hill is etched with patterns made by vanished hands. An archaeological survey conducted twenty years ago recorded almost three hundred relics on the five hundred acres of the common. Some are recent, like the quarries that were used to supply stone for field walls, building and roofing materials. Others are much older. From where I often stand to watch for curlews there are two prehistoric features visible, a ring cairn and a burial mound. Both were emptied long ago. There are other cairns on the hill which I have not yet discovered. They lie intact, the memories they contain still present. Elsewhere there are raised platforms, ditches and embankments, traces of ancient communities which existed here, either in short, warm periods when upland farming could sustain groups of people, or when they were forced to move on to less fertile land.

There is a place on the north-west side of the hill known as Pentre Jack. It can be seen from a distance as an indentation in the slope, a scooped hollow with steep sides overgrown all summer with high bracken. Rainwater drains into a large mawn pool below it. Between the hollow and the pool lie the extensive remains of a medieval settlement. A row of house platforms are clear to see in winter when the bracken has died back. The collapsed walls of small field enclosures surround the platforms, some curving, some straight, following the direction of the slope. The settlement faces west. All winter wind and rain batter the place. Water collects around the walls and for many months the ground is knee-deep in mud. It's a place inhabited only by ravens now. When the wind is gusting they hang in the air high above the slope, then dive down in pairs to be scooped back up, cackling, flipping upside down, folding their wings and extending them to spin and intersect each other's paths. They're tuned to the presence of loss, they know where the ghosts reside.

For years, almost every time I walked on the common there would be an old hill farmer there, feeding cattle in winter, checking lambs and calves in summer. He owned ground on both sides of the common, but, most of the time, left his fields to the spear thistles and sedge. His tiny stone house was falling apart. The porch over the front door had collapsed and its leaning roof was propped with wood so to get in he had to bend his already bent frame. The house had no running water, no indoor toilet. He had been renting it for years because his own home, on the other side of the hill, had become a complete ruin. I sneaked down there one day, walking along a lane of thin mud mixed with sheep shit, bordered on each side by broken walls with hazel and thorn trees growing through them and coils of rusted wire blocking the gaps. Next to the ruin was a metal barn, its corrugated roof part-collapsed, its floor a churn of slurry. In the middle of it were two vets tending to a cow which was lying on its side in the filth, chains attached to its legs, secured to the girders supporting the roof. In the cow's side was a strawberry wound the size of a plate. One of the vets pushed her arms deep into the wound. The old farmer stood at the end of the barn holding on to one of the chains, watching intently as the newest member of his herd was birthed.

I don't know what his land looked like when he was a younger man, but the place had become a portrait of defeat. There was probably too much ground for him to manage, too many animals, too many things falling apart for an old man to continually repair. There are other farms bordering the common in a similar state, managed by elderly farmers who also no longer have the capacity to maintain them. Ancient vehicles litter lanes prowled by half-feral dogs. Farmhouses stand empty, their roofs, walls and windows leaking, repaired carelessly and as cheaply as possible with plastic sheets, corrugated iron, timber offcuts. People live alone in static caravans next to their once-thriving households while ivy twists through gaps in the walls and brambles grow waist-high in the vegetable beds where they used to grow food. Here, the light is fading on a way of life.

To the north of the common is a long limb of exposed upland rising from the banks of the River Wye in rocky steps to a heather and bilberry moor. Near the summit a horseshoe fold in the hill shelters a small farm with a house and attached barn, abandoned decades ago. The barn is leaning, the beams snapped and the roof caved in. The house is missing many of its windows but inside the furniture and fittings – beds, tables, chairs, crockery, rugs, even books and magazines – are still there as if the occupants simply got up one morning, left and forgot to return. The setting for the house is picture-perfect, the house itself a beautiful stone structure fitting perfectly into the landscape, a little paradise that once would have been a mixed farm, filled with life. Cattle, sheep, pigs and poultry would have coexisted alongside crops and a wider landscape of wildflowers, insects and birds. Now the grass-let fields are a uniform, chemically fertilised green right to their wire-fenced edges. There are few insects, few birds. The ghosts are tending to the place now.

The depopulation of rural Wales has been ongoing for a century and a half, and has accelerated in recent decades. The abandonment has been manufactured, deliberately or not, by government policy, corporations and banks. Farm incomes have been choked to the point where small hill farms cannot support the families that live on them. Holdings have been merged into bigger operations and mixed farming practices that supported a rich array of wildlife have disappeared. The memory of these practices is now fading. Their signs in the landscape are starting to disappear, rusted out, ploughed under, becoming part of the archaeology of the place.

I have a friend who has farmed on the hill all his life. He was brought up on a small mixed farm. He remembers when much of the work was done communally. Hedges were laid and maintained by hand, sheep driven to the river to be washed, cows milked and churns left at the farm gate to be collected daily. He remembers cutting hay in the summer with lapwings swooping over the fields and curlew chicks scattering on the ground. He is old now and retired from farming after the foot-and-mouth outbreak in 2001. Last spring a young curlew kept visiting his land, returning every evening to feed in a field near to the farmhouse. It would spook as traffic passed on the lane and fly to another field further up the hill. I watched it for a few weeks, hoping that the bird would return with a mate to nest. But the curlew was alone. It moved on after a time and I never saw it again.

On the side of a track which climbs up to the common there is a small cairn which was once a perfectly shaped dome. On the top was a polished, circular stone with a single initial carved into it. I think it was an M. The cairn is known locally as the Peewit Watcher's Cairn. In my time here it has collapsed and been rebuilt twice. Now it has collapsed again, the stones slowly dispersing, picked up by passing walkers or used to plug ruts in the track. I walked past the monument on my first visit here two decades ago, on a late-spring morning of mist. I had not yet witnessed the big empty spaces of the Welsh uplands and, at first, the place filled me with apprehension. It felt as if I were being watched by a ghostly presence. The drifting mist obscured the features of the common and then revealed them suddenly, curtains parting briefly to show an almost empty stage. When I came to the little cairn I stopped to check the track, which forked at that point. I heard sounds almost like radio static, rising and falling, close and distant. I took the left fork towards the sound and in a few seconds the mist rolled away to reveal a flock of lapwings swooping and diving over the bare ground. I had never seen lapwings before. They were as exotic as any creature I'd ever encountered, as the huge storks and hornbills of Africa, as the gannets and razorbills of Skomer, as the vultures and eagles of the Alps. At that moment the hill became a place of magic. But I only witnessed the flock of lapwings that one time. Since then I've glimpsed them once on the hill, a single pair, high up, flying south. The Peewit Watcher's Cairn is now a tumbled memorial both to the man and the object of his gaze.

*

I'm walking on the hill at dusk, making the most of this lockdown quiet. I've waited by the pool and followed the field walls at the edge of the common looking for curlews, but I haven't seen them yet. Now I'm on my way home, loitering in the transforming light, not yet willing to give up on the birds, hoping for a glimpse of them before dark.

On a plot which slopes away from the common there is an old house which was without a roof for most of the time I've lived here. You can see it from the Peewit Watcher's Cairn. It is situated in the middle ground between the cairn and the slope where I saw the lapwing flock. The house has recently been renovated. An electric gate has been installed and there is a shiny plaque with an uninteresting English name engraved on it. But there's an older name associated with the land it is built on: 'Ty'r Beddau'. It means, the ground of the graves. There is a flat expanse above the house which local memory says was once a battlefield where a thousand Welsh soldiers lost their lives. They were buried here and each grave was marked by an inscribed stone. There is little evidence for this except for the place name and the fact that, a mile north, a battle did take place, at Painscastle, though it was meant to have happened in the immediate location beyond the castle walls. Archaeological digs there have found no remains of the many soldiers that were killed by English forces in that battle. The ground of the graves may be the real location.

It's from behind the roof of the house that the curlews have just appeared, announcing themselves with a high-pitched, single note. They rise now against the background of a partial rainbow floating in front of pewter-dark clouds. They keep rising. Now they're arcing around and coming across the hill, flying up to the crest of a rise topped by a lone thorn tree. As they pass it they turn again and come back towards me, dipping close to the ground, one following the other. They fly over my head, low enough for me to hear the air in their wings, and to see their beaks open as they call again, that long call that undulates like this landscape. They turn, head back to the thorn tree, then turn again. It's rare to see them like this. Usually they rise from the ground as if coming out of it, then quickly land and disappear. But they know that the hill is theirs tonight. The lull in human affairs, caused by a deadly virus, has given the landscape back to them, perhaps for the last time. I'm worried that they'll be lulled by this temporary quiet to let down their guard and nest on the open hill. The sheep will return soon enough, and the horses, tractors and quad bikes, the off-roaders, the dog walkers, fell runners, mountain bikers. I hope that the birds will find a hidden place in a sheltered field which will be left ungrazed until June. Then they'll have a chance.

But now I'm wondering if they're actually here at all. The way they're circling me is so unlike them, how they emerged from a rainbow, out of the graves. This could be my imagination at work, projecting them on to this emptied place where centuries ago wolves hunted and, before them, lions. We are all, at the last, just fading shapes in the memories of others.

JOURNEYS AND MIGRATIONS

My grandfather is walking through a wood at the front edge of dawn. He's tall and has to bend a little to pass beneath the boughs. I can see his hands as he pushes aside a hazel branch, bigger than mine, big knuckles, spade palms, gnarled in the way that hands become after years of manual work. His fingers are stained yellow with nicotine. He is walking in a wood I've been to many times, but never with him. Our tracks have crossed and recrossed. We entered the place through the same gaps and followed the same paths, but we arrived from different places.

Overlooking the wood, only a few hundred metres away, is an A-shaped pit headframe, with its four huge iron wheels. To the west are rows of factories and warehouses. The wood is hemmed in, there isn't a spot inside it where you can't hear engines and wheels. My grandfather worked on the coalface for years until a day when a section of the face collapsed and he was trapped beneath it. His hip and femur were broken in several places and sepsis followed.

He was hospitalised for almost two years and it took several more before he could walk properly again. The coal board then offered him a job above ground driving a tipper truck. The slag heaps and coal dumps that it was his job to maintain bordered the little wood and he walked through it sometimes before his shift. He'd listen to birds and occasionally glimpse foxes in this little wild enclosure, and in the evening he'd tell my mother, who was still a child, about what he'd seen. The sense of wonder she got from those stories passed to me years later and would lead me to search out my own wooded place in the city I could walk to at dawn. The wheels of the headframe were still turning, the cars and trains still speeding past, but once inside I was away from it. I followed animal tracks, peered into burrows and dens, watched the light filter in.

He is pushing away branches with his big hands. The ground is soft and he leaves a shallow footprint with each step. The light has just begun to seep into the spaces beneath the canopy. The trees are mostly birch and sycamore, some ash, some stands of young, scrubby oak. But he's not concerned with the names of trees; he just wants to soak up the atmosphere of this life-filled place which is so different to the other places he knows, the little two-up two-down house he lives in, the narrow alleyways and streets, the blackened factories, bottle kilns and chimney stacks. There is a curtain drawn between him and all those walls for now. The sharp edges of his life have become feathered, and the dust has stopped falling. Instead there is dew.

He can see red in the sky and he sits down on a fallen log to watch it spread. It is painful to sit like this, an ache growing in his hips and creeping down his legs. But he likes it here, so close to the soil. He pulls a pack of cigarettes from his jacket pocket, slides one out and lights it. He takes a drag, fills his lungs. He holds the smoke for a few seconds before tilting his head back and blowing it out, swirling towards the canopy of leaves. He waits, listening to his breath, feeling the breathing of the wood. This silent act of resistance, of resilience, will carry to his children, grandchildren and great-grandchildren. But he has no idea of that. He only knows that this is an important place on the map of his life, a place he needs to circle back to.

*

The sky is deepest blue, the stonework of houses faded to black. There isn't a glowing window in the whole street. We're all listening to and watching the aerial performance of swifts. This is the crescendo and final act. In the coming days the stage will begin to empty and will remain empty for nine long months. The adults and their young are gathered and using the houses to raise the stakes on their stunts, swooping low, almost skimming my hair and hurtling fast towards the walls before tilting a wingtip, flicking on to their sides and catching the little thermals that rise from the roofs, which have been baking in the sun all day. Perhaps the older birds are panting with exhaustion after these two months of furious breeding and foraging for their young. Perhaps the young, just getting to know the abilities of their long, sickle wings, but not quite strong enough yet, are sore and aching as they learn to plummet-dive like their parents. If that is the case, they show no sign of fatigue. The village is a fairground with the fastest rides and I'm watching from the best spot, among the tilting graves of the churchyard, beneath a glowing half-moon.

I burst into tears when I spot my first swift of the year. This is sometimes a dangerous response to a joyful occasion because for several years my first sighting has been on the motorway in rush hour traffic. They often appear low in front of me, skimming above the cars as the road crosses a bridge over the River Wye. I see that first little group of black anchor shapes, my eyes mist up and I simultaneously start laughing. It's a test of the miraculous, this dual response.

I've always wanted to see a bee hummingbird, those tiny hovering jewels, almost impossible to imagine, but real, like the three hearts, nine brains and blue blood of a giant Pacific octopus. The bee hummingbird can comfortably perch on the tip of a child's little finger. It can lay eggs in a thimble. It can drink nectar from the tiniest flowers, hovering above them while its topaz wings beat invisibly and silently. The word miracle has evolved from Old French and Latin – *miraculum* – *mirari* – *mirus* – words which meant 'to wonder'. Its earlier form, derived from Proto-Indo-European, was the word *smeiros*, which meant 'to smile or laugh'. The word it replaced in Old English was *wundorweorc*. Possibly I never will see a bee hummingbird, but swifts are from the same family and they're also wonderworks.

The light is changing above them, all Earth's colours turning ochre. In a few minutes the helter-skelter aerobatics will wind down and the swifts will start to climb high into the sky, two or three kilometres up. This is theoretically when they shut down half of their brains at a time, each half alternating between sleep and wakefulness during their descent, which, even at those heights, does not take more than a few seconds. Their frog mouths shut, their huge eyes close one at a time, their wings lock into position for the spiralling downslide. When a swift leaves its nest it will be on the wing for up to ten months, a period when it will only sleep for a few minutes a day, the rest of its time spent in a fury of activity as it follows clouds of insects south across Europe and then into Africa.

Across the street from the churchyard is the old house where Francis Kilvert lived while he was curate here, between 1865 and 1872, and where he wrote his diaries filled with closely observed descriptions of rural life. In the whole collection of over a hundred thousand words he doesn't mention swifts once, and only refers to swallows twice, on both occasions as a summer nuisance. In his time farms required a lot of human labour. There were many rough-built houses with mudstone roofs and draughty gable ends able to host nesting swifts. And there were insects in vast numbers: 'Sunday, 8 August. As I went to Church in the sultry summer afternoon the hum and murmur of the multitudinous insects sounded like the music of innumerable bells.' This place had far more wild inhabitants back then. Was the gentle curate less curious than he's taken to be? How did he not find room in his diaries for swifts? He must have sat here, where I'm sitting now, with the low branches of an old yew tree swaying a little in the breeze, while perhaps hundreds of swifts plummet-dived and screeched over the rooftops. Since his time industrialisation has squeezed the life from the place. What I'm witnessing is a shred, a tatter of what he saw. Only the moon remains as it was then, and the urgency of wild things.

Uncontrollable laughing and crying have always felt the same to me, the chest convulsions, the location of them, inside and outside of the body, as if something like a cloud has descended, not on you, but through you. The feeling, after it has overtaken you, that you might not be the composer of your own life, or even the musician, but just the plucked, strummed or blown instrument. You're picked up, shaken, put down. Those same hands have just reached into a nest where a swift is doing press-ups with its newly fledged wings. The hand has lifted it quickly, pulled the little ball of almost weightless flesh and feathers out into the twilight and thrown it hard into the sky. Already the little creature is screaming and merging its voice with the flock. Already it is flicking and twist-diving over the church tower, hurtling out and rounding the Scots pines and skimming the old forge roof, then up and over the oaks and the rooks' nests. Within a few seconds it has completed its first circuit of the village and is out over the sheep fields, over the main road, the millstream and pond. Then back again and round again, and again. It has no idea where it's going and is not looking for anything to follow. It's not fearful or excited, though its mouth is gaping. It will always be hungry. It climbs a chimney of air then rolls and plummets back as the rectangles of the houses, the dark clouds of the trees, the little pebbles of the gravestones grow and grow. Its huge eyes take in the face of a human creature staring up at it, and then the creature is gone behind the walls and fences, the hedges, the ancient castle mound. For the past weeks it has been staring into the dark of the nest, now it is seeing the dying fire of daylight for the first of many times as the sky swings and revolves.

Perhaps time existed for the bird while it grew into this form, while it fed continuously, the days and nights long with waiting. But now time has stopped and there is only air and speed, the transforming light, the broken chequerboard map of the landscape which will soon change as it heads south, turning dark blue as it crosses the sea, brown, red and gold over the mountains and desert. It will see streams, rivers, hills and dunes undulating in a fierce light, deep shadows, lands that have not been cut into pieces but flow as a whole. Each night as it heads south it will see the sky more clearly, speckled with light, spattered with light, running with a river of light, lamplit by the moon. Eventually it will find the rains and follow them for months or even years, until the urge comes to head north again. For now it is taking in the cool currents of the sky, the moon, the taste of flying insects. It will spend the next day or two configuring its senses, feeling the path of the sun, the draw of warmth and the push of cold.

In the churchyard the yew trees have turned black. A first bat is buffeting and rebounding around the church, its little leather wings audible in the almost silence. The swifts are climbing now, in spirals as wide as the village, shrinking to tiny slits in the deep sky. One, two, three, four cross the face of the moon and now I can't see them. I don't know why I feel so sad. I don't know why I'm laughing.

*

The plane has just turned to face a wide and arrow-straight runway. I'm gripping the arm rests, sweat trickling down my back. Flying, to me, is the least natural act a human being can undertake. It makes no sense that this winged tube of aluminium, which is already flexing and groaning, can carry so many people so high and so far. It is the least birdlike of things. Now we are accelerating, the engines loud, the wheels hitting the sections of tarmac more and more quickly. We're in the air somehow and the plane seems to drop rather than rise. I'm staring out of a tiny window, watching the sun sink behind the airport terminal and cityscape, which shrinks back and becomes a map of itself. The plane climbs, then banks left, the sun swivelling out of view. At altitude twilight lasts for hours. Already the clouds are rippling with fire below us and space is a speckled sea. If we're lucky we'll reach Greenland in a clear sky, with icebergs shining beneath us. Then Baffin Island and the Canadian North glowing with frozen luminescence.

Our brains fizz with activity even when our minds are quiet, eighty billion neurons lighting up intermittently, sending signals across a network that resembles the electric nightscape of London, New York or Beijing. But at dusk the background activity quietens. The visual cortex and the auditory and somatosensory regions reduce their signals at this time, allowing us to detect slighter stimuli. This is a common attribute in animals and one that humans have not lost. The body tunes itself to perceive more as the light fades. But though this dusk is one of the longest I've encountered, my body is not tuned to it at all. It is cut off, desensitised, encapsulated by the protective atmosphere. We're moving at two-thirds the speed of sound through hurricane-strength winds at minus fifty degrees and we sense none of it. On a plane my ears seem to malfunction. They whirr, chatter and whistle. Voices drift over me clumped together like an auditory fog with occasional spikes as if the volume has been suddenly turned up. I struggle to converse, even with the person sitting next to me. The grey light seems sourceless, shadows are faint and I have to touch things to make sure they're three-dimensional. My skin, in this place without wind or even the slightest temperature fluctuation, goes numb. A plane is not a good place for organisms.

In the early era of transcontinental flight in America journeys were slow and unreliable. Mail pilots had no on-board navigation equipment. To improve flight times the US government built huge concrete platforms every few miles right across the country. They were created in the shape of an arrow and painted bright yellow to help with visibility. They then fixed metal towers with rotating lights to the arrows. Pilots would follow these beacons, one to the next, to stay on track. During the Second World War, when aircraft were fitted with internal navigation systems, the towers were dismantled and the metal recycled for the war effort. The concrete platforms remained. Arrow hunting is now a pastime. People search for them in deserts, mountains and other wild regions in order to photograph them. Most are hidden, cracked, overgrown with weeds and trees, hosts to lichens.

The plane is starting its descent. I feel the first slide down the air, like being dropped on to a deep cushion. Outside I can see the dust-speck lights of farms. As we descend the specks become constellations, then pointillist clusters joined by long straight lines. When the city comes into view an umber haze appears and the faintest trace of the horizon. The points of light below start to move into and out of cloud haze like the edges of a huge phosphorescent creature. Grids and angled intersections appear, rooftops and roads. We're re-entering the machine. The shapes are familiar and the familiarity grows, lights become windows and screens, illuminated billboards filled with pictures we've seen thousands of times before that follow us everywhere. As the wing dips and we turn, the shining path of the runway comes into view, identical to the one we left hours ago. I feel the whirr and clunk of the landing gear, then another descending lunge, and another. Now the city buildings are not below me, but on every side, empty and glowing. We're thousands of miles from home in a place that looks familiar.

That long-haul flight made me feel like I'd never left home, but the meandering journey that followed seems so important to me now. In the mountainous west of Canada I travelled through a landscape that showed me what my own northern land was once like, an ecosystem humming with life. I saw blue lakes, rivers filled with salmon, uncut forests inhabited by bears, wolverines, lynxes, all extinct in my own country. I would also witness the melting of glaciers up-close, touching calved icebergs fallen from glacial formations that were once branched and shaped like birds' feet, now shrunk to blunt stumps. There were roads lined with logging trucks, whole valleys clear-felled of primary-growth trees. In the little rural towns there were stores filled with hunting rifles, the heads of animals proudly displayed. I walked into a grocery shop one day where the almost black skin of a wolf was splayed across the wall above the counter. The next day I would meet one face to face.

*

It only takes a week for a swift to travel from my home in Wales to the Gulf of Guinea. It could take multiple routes. It could keep to the western seaboards of Europe and Africa. Or it could choose to cross the Mediterranean and follow a more direct route over the Algerian and Malian deserts, down through Burkina Faso, and Niger, the way of the ancient traders and salt caravans. Many birds travel to the Congo where they follow its great river-sea into the heart of Africa. Here they overwinter, feeding in areas where insect concentrations are at their most dense. Some make it to eastern Congo, then follow routes down Lake Kivu into Tanzania, flying all the way to the Indian Ocean, before circling back to the rainforest. As the urge to breed begins again, they head west and north, often taking quite different routes to the ones that brought them south. In the whole of Africa no roosting site has even been found for common swifts. When tracked with geolocators over a full year cycle some swifts were found not to have landed on a single occasion outside of the breeding period.

Swifts drink by catching raindrops in mid-air, or sweeping down and taking single sips from the surface of a pool, stream or river. They follow watercourses and avoid storms by navigating around them or flying straight into the wind to get through them as fast as they can. They feed on thousands of species of insect, following plumes and hatching swarms, aerial plankton blown up to a kilometre high. They are perhaps Earth's greatest journeyers. In a lifespan that averages twenty years they travel the distance to the moon and back seven times. A swift needs no landmarks, no coordinates, it feels its way electromagnetically along the circles, ovals and figures of eight it scribbles over continents, recalibrating fractionally at dawn and dusk. Though it spends most of its life traversing the equator it feels the slow changes of Earth to the north, the sun's waxing and waning, the coming and going of the cold. In a flock of swifts seen over the Congo River in December, some birds will have hatched in Cardiff or Oxford, Paris or Geneva, Moscow or Saint Petersburg, Kathmandu or Beijing, a furious multiculture, each adapted identically, but orientated differently. No swift ever travels from one destination to another tracking a straight line. There is no beginning or end for them, only the summer dawn of awakening, the continuous flickering journey over ever-changing landscapes: plains and hills, oceans and rivers, wetlands, deserts, forests, lakes, islands. Every year, at the end of April, I watch for them. They arrive, coming upstream, diving under the bridge, sweeping back over it and between the hanging willows, frenzied, on the move, urgent with intent to breed, to gyrate above the valley for a too-short time, before their journey continues.

*

I'm gathering traces of a journey across Africa made half my lifetime ago. All I have is a piece of bark cloth and a worn map. Both have been locked away for decades. I remember clearly the man who gave me the cloth. He lived deep in the Congo forest, hundreds of miles from the nearest town. He was dressed in ragged Western clothes – a T-shirt with a rip through the chest, a pair of shorts which must have once belonged to a child. He was no bigger than a child. I remember he had skin which was finely creased and shiny; that he didn't smile; that he carried a bow and a quiver of arrows; that he came out of the trees on to a road which was cratered and flooded, emerging like a ghost. When he stepped back into the forest he vanished into the twilight beneath the canopy.

The cloth he gave me is torn and creased, with a cross-hatched, blur-edged pattern. I can't remember what I gave him for it. It may have been a pen. We didn't know a single word of each other's language. We gesticulated, mimed. He was polite, but disinterested, trading an object that must have taken time to make for something he had little use for. Because the piece of cloth was easy to stow it travelled with me for many months, and I eventually brought it home. It has barely been touched since.

I'm unfolding it now. It has not faded, but it feels ancient. A crease down the centre is a stiff ridge and the weave is loose. On either side of the crease are different patterns. On one side it is geometric with vertical stripes punctuated by perpendicular, ladder-shaped cross-strokes. Like trunks and branches. On the other a pattern is formed from loose triangles with misshapen rectangles attached to them. Like twigs and leaves. The culture of the people who crafted the cloth was as ancient as those that built the cairns and standing stones on the hills above my home. They were still hunter-gatherers, though their way of life was being infiltrated and threatened. In the years since, I've read about the continual decimation of the Congo. The patterns on the cloth now represent to me rows of felled trees, logs floated in huge rafts down the great river, decimated landscapes inhabited by displaced people.

The map I carried on the journey is fragile now, the paper heavily foxed, each crease a dark brown line that tears a little as it unfolds. I have to open it carefully. The name Zaire is printed across the centre in gold lettering, a name that no longer exists. The great river, then also called Zaire, arcs across the sheet, its huge tributaries branching blue through the pale green of the rainforest, like a sea fan leaning away from the tide. I read the names of those tributaries: Momboyo, Ikelemba, Lulonga, Salonga, Tshuapa. The section of forest where I met the pygmy hunter is the size of a coin, unnamed, only the mud road that cut through it marked with a red dotted line. I no longer recognise the names of the villages I must have passed through, Adusa, Mambasa, Apawanza, but I remember the road, almost impassable in places, with craters feet deep and full to the brim with flood water. We had to bail out those craters by hand using buckets, then dig out the slurry beneath to allow vehicles to pass through. It took days to travel a few miles.

There was nothing in the landscape to navigate with, no landmarks, no horizon, only the overhanging trees. When I passed through a village there were no signs to show its name. I opened the map each day and tried to guess where I was. Sometimes I wandered into the forest a little way from the road to pitch my tent and spent the night listening to the shrieking calls of animals I could not identify. I'd wake up in the morning totally disorientated, the road hard to find. Occasionally I would come across a hill or mound that I could climb and reach a spot high enough to look out across the canopy, which continued in every direction without a single break, a circle of dark green. I was travelling inside an organism.

For the pygmies, wayfinding was not a case of reading maps, but knowing what was being communicated by the trees. It must take multiple generations to learn to read a place that way, a desire to travel slowly, to take winding paths and wide circles. After I got home from that journey I realised I'd seen little of Africa, only a thin thread strung west to east, as wide as my gaze, which, in the rainforest, was only a few metres. This is how most of our travels go, moving through narrow corridors, unable to weave like swifts, unable to get to know the terrain.

*

I've been following wild horses at dusk. There are small herds on every hill and mountain common in this area, left untouched for most of their lives. They are not easy to approach, moving away from you as soon as you get close enough to see the mud on their coats. You can push a trained horse away from you with your eyes, and pull it back with a bow of your head. But not a wild one. At dusk though they're less guarded, and you can get close to them if you're careful. The task is to be invisible for as long as possible.

I see the herd grazing a patch of ground near to the pool, their grey to white coats holding the failing light. There is little cover here, only low-growing bracken and sprays of gorse. I follow a track where a runnel of water descends from a spring, the soft ground soaking up the sound of my feet. As I move closer I can hear the horses ripping at the grass. I step forward more slowly. They still haven't felt my presence, so I sit at this distance and watch until the sky is almost completely dark and I can only just make out their silhouettes. I stand again and step closer, not quite knowing where each horse is now, their shapes blending with the dark. When the light is this low I somehow see more through the tails of my eyes, making out the arched shoulders of the stallion to my left, the flicking tail of a mare whose foal is close to her. Now I am standing in the middle of the herd and they still haven't noticed me. I can hear their velvet breathing, their twitches and soft grunts. But somehow I have tripped the wire. A head snaps up and a horse snorts. I step back, but it's too late. They spook as one, turn and fly. The ground is drumming as they gallop away along the tracks between the bracken. In seconds they're out of sight, over the brow of the hill, which I can only just faintly see, the sound of their hooves rapidly fading.

Tracking herds is one of the skills humans developed early in our evolution. It's as ancient as building fires or knapping flint. There have been many theories about what makes nomads decide to move from one place to another. Some anthropologists believe that it is a homeostatic act, seeking to preserve the surrounding environment. Others think it is economic, that movement is motivated by trade in order to create social opportunities, to barter goods or facilitate new relationships and marriages. In recent studies of Nenet and Komi reindeer herders in northern Russia old herders were asked why they chose to move at a certain time to a particular place. The herders were surprised by the question. They told the researchers that they didn't make decisions, they simply followed the reindeer. But as the researchers studied them over their annual cycles they realised that decisions were being made, based on centuries-old knowledge. After being so close to the animals for so long, the herders could feel instinctively when the reindeer would move and to where. They weren't driving them, but they could anticipate the herd and effectively be part of it. Perhaps this is the way that the human species spread across the continents, following the animals as they navigated the world for us.

*

I think I can hear the screaming of birds, faintly, distantly, over the miles and miles of forest canopy. I'm in the back of an ancient truck piled high with sacks of food, fresh yams, mangos, pineapples, plantains, bananas. Between the sacks people are perched as best they can to stay upright as the vehicle smashes into ruts in the mud road. We've been travelling all day and everyone is tired. The smell of rotting fruit and human sweat is thick beneath the canvas canopy. I've been hitching lifts with trucks for days now, trying to find my way to the Kahuzi-Biega National Park in eastern Congo, to see mountain gorillas. But it is still far away and I'm not quite sure how I'll get there. A little boy, maybe six years old, is less tolerant of the discomfort than the rest of us. He shuffles continually and talks to his grandmother, who is sitting beside a new bicycle, its chrome wheels and handlebars glinting. Occasionally the boy stares at me and I pull the corners of my mouth wide, grimacing, crossing my eyes. He pulls the same face back, giggles, then quickly, shyly, looks away. The truck begins to slow, gears crashing as we see a line of tin-roofed buildings appear. The back door is lowered and people start to climb out. I shoulder my rucksack.

The village is just a row of mud brick compounds lining either side of the road. As I start to look for somewhere to stay the sun drops rapidly, flaring out its refracted light against high cirrus and cirrostratus clouds. I can see the waves of hilltops and beyond those the cone of a volcano, green almost to its summit. The forest's deep emerald is washed to burnt umber as the sky rushes through the spectrum before tropical night swarms out of the soil beneath ebony, mahogany, limba and iroko trees. As the world fades I see dark fragments high above me, swifts, recently arrived from Europe, sweeping over the forest in large numbers, glutting on insects. A group breaks off and skids above the street, before twisting out over the rusted rooftops to disappear against the canopy.

There is nowhere to stay in this place, and no yard or field to pitch a tent. My only choice is to hike into the forest and find a spot under the trees where I'll be eaten alive by mosquitos and kept awake all night by the hundred-decibel screams of tree hyraxes. I walk to the end of the village, turn around and walk back. In the last light I see the twinkling of chrome on the wheels of a bicycle. The old woman and her grandson are waiting. As I approach, the boy grabs my hand and they lead me through a gate, into a yard with a tiny house in its centre. A faint glow undulates from a candle placed on a windowsill. They guide me inside and I sit on a wooden chair facing a sofa which slowly fills with curious children and their mother. I only know a few words of Swahili and they know no English. We gesticulate, laughing at the sounds of the strange words we voice, the names we can't pronounce. The old woman leads me into the yard where she has built a fire and heated water for me to wash. When I go back into the house there is sugary tea, goat stew, tomatoes. The children approach me with more courage as the hours pass. They reach out to touch my strange hair, its texture making them shiver, and they screech with laughter as they run back to their mother. Their grandmother shoos them away and beckons to me to follow her out of the room and across the yard to a mud-floored hut filled with beds. She points to a bed I can use and leaves me, closing the rickety door behind her. Through a ripped curtain in a window only half-glazed I can see the glow cast by the fire in the yard where she is heating more water. I lie on the bed and fall asleep.

I wake to a grey rectangle, hanging in dark space like a Rothko piece. As I stare it seems to vibrate against the background, as if its edges can't bear the touch of darkness. Then the lines of the iron bed frames begin to draw themselves. Birds are beginning to sing, in those voices that have surprised me every morning since I arrived on this continent, strange and exotic. Mixing with them are the familiar shrieks of swifts. In the half-light I stand and manoeuvre through gaps between the beds, then pull the door open to get a better view of the dawn. Directly opposite me, lying on the ground, wrapped in a dusty blanket and without a pillow, the old woman is sleeping. Her daughter and grandchildren are also asleep, in a line against the mud-brick wall. They have slept outside to give me the privacy of their only bedroom.

I don't remember the name of the old woman. I don't remember her face, or her hands. I don't remember the sound of her voice, or how she spoke to her grandchildren. I don't remember the colour of the bicycle she pushed along the road, or how she decorated her home. Did she have flowers in the windows? Were there pictures on the walls, gathered objects, mementos from her life? The harder I try to remember, the less I can see, like an image after dark, a shape that moves on the periphery of my sight, then disappears when I turn to it. I only remember what she did for me, how her act of generosity became a landmark in my life which led me to my own acts of hospitality, to other people, and to other species. And swifts, I remember the swifts.

It is three days since I left the house where the old woman and her family slept in the yard. I've travelled fast, having discovered an airfield in the forest, a battered plane going south which I managed to get a seat in. After that a boat journey across Lake Kivu and a predawn taxi ride have brought me to Kahuzi-Biega National Park and I'm now on foot for a much slower journey up a steep mountainside. The trunks of trees are faint. Beyond is the lake, wide as a sea. An hour ago, while I waited in the predawn chill, the full moon descended into it, the tail of its reflection like a comet's. Now it is a field of blue-black. The trail we are following is almost invisible to me and the guides are walking too fast up this steep path. I trip every few steps, my feet hitting roots and vines. I'm told to be quiet. There are forest elephants nearby. If they see us they may charge. The guides carry what look like sticks of dynamite in their pockets, explosive flairs that will, hopefully, scare any aggressive elephant away. I hear the whirr of beetle wings, the high-pitched hum of mosquitos passing close to my ears.

Dawn flows into the spaces between branches. Even here on the equator, where the sun leaps into the sky, the light moves into the forest slowly. The forest appears in wash over wash of intensifying green. The soundscape transforms from the haunting ghost calls of night to the rippling orchestra of morning. We pass lines of ants crossing the path in military formation and see the silhouettes of chimpanzees high in the canopy. The understorey becomes denser as we climb. There are stands of alpine bamboo, fans of ferns, vine tendrils strung over everything. After hours of climbing we come across a flattened area on the ground, soiled with faeces, the first sign. The guides are now making soft groans and huffs. A row of bamboo spears shake. And then they appear, right in front of us, as if they'd been there all along, waiting for us to notice. Two jet-black figures stare at us with an utter lack of concern. They lounge in the weeds, comfortable as royals.

A rapid drumming sound comes from just up the hill. The silverback is making his presence known. He is sitting in the half-light beneath a dense thicket of young trees, a shadow form, double-sumo-sized, his short, tree-trunk legs crossed in front of him. He holds his fist up to his face and slowly splays his fingers, then pokes one into his mouth and twists out the sodden remains of a leaf. He rolls forward and I see the shimmer of the pale fur on his back like light bouncing off a pool. The guides are speaking to him in a half-language, Swahili words mixed with moans and low growls. They keep their heads bowed, almost reverent. As he moves towards us his silver hairs spark and glisten, his eyes shadowed beneath his enormous protruding brow. He's close enough now that I can hear his breath, which is whistling slightly. He strides past me, close enough for me to almost reach out and touch him, but that is not something I would dare to attempt. His fur is raked in places, tangled in others, burrs and tiny twigs stuck to it. A female comes to him at a run, then circles him and they both lope downhill out of sight. We pause for a moment, then follow.

When we catch sight of him again he is lying on his side in the dim beneath bushes. Again we approach slowly. He rolls over and the female appears. She pushes forward. He positions himself directly behind her and mounts her. They watch us nonchalantly as they mate. Their ease with this lack of privacy is perhaps a sign of hospitality. In this place of fragmented light, where a silverback gorilla can vanish only a few feet from us and even elephants go undetected, it seems strange that they don't withdraw. Other people in the group are taking photographs, camera motor drives whirring. But I feel like an intruder now. I walk away to watch and listen to the forest.

This place is the most pristine wilderness I will ever witness. I want to be part of the whole of it for a time. I like the way the trees cocoon the warm air and stain the light. I like the chorus of sounds and smells. Surrounding me are more species than I've ever encountered, hidden beneath the canopy or flying above it: colobus monkeys, blue monkeys, owl-faced monkeys and mangabeys; bongos, duikers and forest buffalos; bush squirrels, water civets, needle-clawed galagos; turacos, sunbirds, broadbills and crimsonwings. There are over 300 species of bird and 130 mammals in the area, and thousands of species of plant occupying highland and lowland ecosystems. It is one of the most ecologically rich areas in the world, the most fiercely alive of places. It feels like home.

Only a few miles from the place where I stood in the presence of gorillas, ancient hostilities between two peoples had recently rekindled, though I had little awareness of it at the time. The rainforest which borders the Congo and Rwanda, the home of most of the tiny population of mountain gorillas, had become a hiding place for militias beginning a brutal conflict which would eventually lead to the death of a million people in Rwanda and fan out across the region, sparking the even more brutal Congo War. Almost six million people died as a result of that conflict, most from malnutrition and starvation, the biggest loss of life since the Second World War.

Goma and Bukavu, the towns at the north and south ends of the lake, both small when I visited, have now swollen into huge, refugee-filled cities. The surrounding area has been logged, burned and farmed to support the population. The gorillas, who once lived in a forest which stretched across the whole of Central Africa, now inhabit green islands, surrounded by farms and roads which transport raw materials from open-cast mines, extracting the vast mineral wealth of the area: cobalt, copper, tantalum, tin, diamonds and gold. These are carried to the coast and exported to factories where they are used in a huge range of our technologies including nuclear reactors, missiles and aircraft parts.

As a species we've grown our numbers 50 per cent in the three decades since I met the gorillas, adding almost three billion to the five we were then. In 2020 a survey estimated the total population of mountain gorillas to be a thousand. We outnumber our sister species eight million to one.

The words hospitality and hostility have the same root, the Proto-Indo-European word *ghos-ti*, meaning guest, stranger and also host, a person with reciprocal duties towards others. It was an important concept in ancient society. But because of the nature of host–guest relationships and how these can become fraught, the word took diverging paths. In English the result is two opposing words. One leads to friendship, the other to war. In the case of hostility to other species it leads to extinction.

I am looking at a photograph of a silverback gorilla lying on its back, arms extended above its head, eyes closed. The legs are bent and spread, the great hands curled loosely into fists. It has a peaceful look, the usually knotted eyebrows soft and relaxed. Behind it, in a row, are six other gorillas similarly posed, females and juveniles. All of them are lying on stretchers created from bamboo poles, ropes around their wrists, ankles and waists. The silverback is being carried by a group of fifteen men through a field of corn. In 2007, this group of gorillas in Virunga National Park, north of Goma, were found dead by rangers after they heard gunshots in the forest the previous night. The silverback had eight bullet wounds in its back. They had been killed by members of a militia who were controlling the trade of charcoal, which is the main source of cooking fuel in the nearby city. The motive behind the killings was that if the forest was cleared of its gorilla population there would be no further need to protect it and therefore more trees could be cut down and processed for charcoal. The men in the photograph were risking their lives carrying the gorillas. In a two-decade period 120 park wardens have been murdered while trying to protect the apes. For humans and wildlife this area of Africa became the least hospitable place on the planet, a conflict zone avoided by the rest of the world, inhabited only by those who had nowhere else to go.

On my return from Kahuzi-Biega, hitching a ride on the back of a truck, I passed a village loomed over by the smoking cone of Mount Nyiragongo. On the side of the road a few men and children stood holding out pineapples and mangos, dried fish and cooked meat to sell. A man in a ripped shirt had a little black bundle in his arms. As the truck got closer the little bundle became an infant chimpanzee, tiny as a six-month-old child, beautiful and terrified. The man held it out to me in an attempted sale. I shook my head and passed by, one of the lucky ones who had a road to follow, a border to cross, an escape route.

*

It is summer's dawn. I'm listening to birdsong over the village, the fury of the breeding season under way. Today I'm up just before the sun, though I won't see it rise, the cloud is thick and low, smoking on the hills. I'm walking through the churchyard under thick yews, past Kilvert's house and the stream which runs underneath the garden to emerge from a tunnel on the edge of the road. Light into dark into light. I cross the road and enter a field overlooking a wide floodplain which has been transformed in recent years into a thousand monocrop acres bordering the river, hedges ripped out, every inch ploughed in parallel rows, planted with potatoes and rapeseed. The plain would once have provided winter grazing for animals managed in an ancient transhumance system, where livestock spent summers grazing the high ground and winters sheltered in lowland pastures. A few weeks ago it was a glistening lake created by an Atlantic low which brought so much rain to the valley that the roads were cut off for days.

The floodplain below the village runs parallel to the upland common. The two areas are connected via many narrow lanes and tracks that were used to move livestock between summer and winter pastures. The lanes have transformed from lack of use. In summer they become weed-infested and overgrown with thorns. In winter they turn into streams that carve an ever-deeper track downhill. Some have been erased by bulldozers, planted over and incorporated into fields. There is one lane which is still used occasionally. All year it is a secret road for foxes, polecats, badgers, otters. I'm heading there now, over the fields, along the river, travelling slowly, the way my ancestors did, on the move but staying home. I cross the empty road, take the track that winds steeply down to the river through a stand of horse chestnuts luminous with new leaf. There is a scream above the trees, then another, high-pitched and furious. I rush out into the clearing beside the water and see three dark anchors high in the sky, speeding upriver. The swifts are here. They turn and rush back, skimming above the weir, behind them invisible trails created over months of non-stop flying, scribbled from the Wye to the Congo. For a while they'll be following the same tracks that I follow, circling the village while each dusk almost touches dawn. They'll measure the light until, with the members of their new broods now grown and able to navigate, the darkness each side of day will come too close, and the nomads will be gone again.

I'm walking more and more, following the same tracks from the valley bottom up to the summit of the hill, along the ridge, then back, a transhumance of sorts. Anxiety is forcing me to follow this circular path continually.

Just before a big storm Julia, who had been recovering over the winter and spring from pulmonary embolisms, and slowly adapting to diabetes, became suddenly ill again, a headache getting worse, her speech becoming slurred and her right side weak. An ambulance sped her thirty miles to the hospital and I followed in the car, having been told by a paramedic that she was having a stroke.

When I arrived I was directed to a waiting room in the resuscitation ward where I sat alone for the longest hour of my life, listening to the muffled voices of nurses through the wall, urgent among the birdlike sounds of medical equipment. A cleaner walked in and offered to make me tea, almost in tears as she asked. I don't know how many times a day the route she followed through the labyrinthine hospital took her to meet others waiting to find out if their loved ones had survived. While I was there the storm set in. Trees were blowing down, rain falling so hard it washed the topsoil from fields turning the surface of the roads into slurry. The river was rising.

I was eventually told that Julia had been taken to the ward upstairs to be monitored. Though the stroke had been mild there was a very high chance of another happening in the following hours which could be more severe. I was shown to her bedside. We held hands, watched the comings and goings of the hospital staff, stared out of the window at an empty courtyard, lead clouds above it, the wind gyrating, lifting plumes of dust, chocolate wrappers and crisp packets four storeys into the air, like swifts at dusk. As I sat there my thoughts gyrated. Where was this journey taking us? When would it end?

Every moment of every day since I have been in a state of hypervigilance. The chance of another stroke reduces with each passing week but Julia has had so many complications since her cancer diagnosis I've come to the conclusion that her journey back to health is going to be very long and filled with life-threatening obstacles looming out of the dark. All I can do is wait, watch, walk.

*

A friend called yesterday to say she had seen a pair of curlews by the pool, so I'm out early, following the edges of the common, peering through my binoculars, scanning the bordering fields and listening hard. I see crows and starlings, a distant red kite, a redstart on the field wall, but no signs of the curlews. Perhaps I won't be lucky today. The pool is quiet, inhabited by a trio of meandering coots and a pair of mallards.

There is a small bowl shape in the turf at my feet. Though the grass is dun brown, this little indentation is so green it seems almost luminescent. To see the source of this colour I kneel and pick out a strand of weed, a long hair's-width root trailing from tiny opposed leaves. It grows on the common wherever there is a spring, the first markers for the watershed on this side of the hill. All over the common there are green tracks in the ground where rainwater collects. Some have been made by the runoff from springs, others by sheep which have carved routes across the hillside with their feet. The tracks collect and form wider streams lower down which merge and cut deeper.

At the edge of a field, which the curlews sometimes visit, two streams meet and roll over a miniature waterfall, through a plantation of conifers. From there it steps down faster, cutting through a wooded ravine which I visit often. A boggy path leads into it. The trees there are starved of light and the trunks grow high and thin fighting each other to reach the canopy. Many snap and collapse, blocking the way. The stream races downhill. I often follow it, sliding over little races and steps, over smooth and slippery rocks into icy pools. There are wild orchids, huge hart's tongue ferns, and bracket fungi, as big as plates, protruding from tree trunks. Birdsong ripples through the leaves. It is the wildest place in this valley.

Inside the wood there is an old gate and beyond it an overgrown yard bordered by ruined stone walls so mossed over and coated with epiphytes that almost no stone is visible. The remains of a cottage stand in the yard, hollowed to a roofless shell with a fireplace choked with nettles and ferns. An oak lintel supports the doorless doorway, the pattern of its grain deeply etched out by years of rain. Across from the house there is an abandoned flatbed trailer almost rusted into the earth. Its bed is a trap for leaves which have rotted down and become soil for ferns and wildflowers, a garden on wheels. Radiating out from the house are rows of narrow terraces supported by stone walls. It must have been hard to survive in this place, and in the end it was abandoned. Here is a view of the past and future, land cut out of the wild, used for generations, then taken back, the way everything we humans take will eventually be reclaimed. A plume of life flows through the little wood, within its green walls it hums with insects and birds. Below the wood the stream runs into the River Wye and becomes part of a wide channel winding between the low hills over the English border before it twists back into Wales to flow into the slow-moving, silty waters of the Severn and the in-reaching sea.

I don't know how long it takes for the rainwater which weeps out of the little springs on the high common to reach the sea. What connects both ends of its journey are the curlews. They spend their winters skirting the muddy tidal edges of the Severn Estuary, together with birds that summer thousands of miles away. Then, when the urge to breed comes, a few, now only a precious few, follow the river upstream to this valley while the rainwater that has fallen here many times before falls again. All the tracks that lead to this place, to every place, trace circles within circles.

LIGHT ON WATER

Lately, as part of Julia's recovery, we've been spending time on a narrowboat. The windows are small and let in little light. Nights are chill and damp, an almost-mist hovering inside. We leave the hatches open so we can listen to the sounds of the river, which is slow and silty, opaque and secretive, winding between the meadows, orchards and wooded hills.

Today I've come to the boat to be alone, my hermitage. It is sparsely equipped. There is no hot water, and the lighting is connected to batteries that never seem to charge. There is little space, I bang my head every time I stand up. I have only the trees and water birds for company. At dusk I watch the willows shifting as their leaves darken into the folding night. I listen to the rushing of the weir downstream, to soft rain against the roof. The boat rocks gently when I move, slows and stills. I open the hatches to listen and watch the quieting of the birds as they begin to roost. The warblers in the reeds are the first to hush, and the mallards, which have been towing their chicks backwards and forwards across the water for hours, slide into hiding. The raucous sound of little grebes, which I have not seen once all day, rattles out. The rooks in a nearby stand of oaks shoal into the sky and spin back, not wanting the day to end just yet. Finally they calm and go silent. There is a blackbird calling to another across the water, and a robin still abroad, martins skipping across the surface to hawk insects for the last time. Then they're gone. As I sit back and watch the outline of trees against the almost-night sky a parade of Canada geese paddle upstream double file, young chaperoned by parents and a cabal of fussing relatives. There is a lone swan on the water. It follows the geese for a while then circles and glides into the reeds calling its soft, plaintive call.

Twilight over water seems to hold a deeper stillness, as if the river or the sea, the lake or pool, is drawing time into itself. It asks us to slow down, to mull things over, to ruminate on the poetry of a day, of a life, to tease out the metaphors and meanings. The fading light is an ending and beginning, the place where the straight lines we attempt to measure our lives with arc and become circles. It's easier to see the flow of things at dusk, to see what's there even as it becomes hidden from view.

*

I don't know how many times I've looked down at this ring of water. It has become as familiar to me as the faces of my children, and as readable. I've watched it appear out of the darkness at dawn and fade back into it at dusk. I've watched it glitter silver at noon and glow copper at sunset. I've seen it frozen solid and covered with half a metre of snow, and I've seen the snow melt, the ice fracture into plates and splinters with swans gliding in between. I've seen flowers come up from its shallow bottom and spread right across the surface, transforming it into a yellow meadow, and then a month later watched them wilt and die back, then sink down to become the silt from which the next year's bloom will grow. There have been many birds. The always-present coots that stay here right up to the freeze, nodding rapidly across the water from one reed patch to the next. The mallards, swans, tufted ducks and teal that arrive in spring. The black-headed gulls that appear at the same time, noisy neighbours, twitchy birds which seem to carry as much anxiety as I do. Buzzards and red kites are ever-present. There is a single kestrel which lingers here in early autumn and which I follow across the hill, trying to get a close look, but never can as it flicks away from me, always maintaining its distance. I've seen two merlins hunting over the pool, an occasional peregrine and once, fleetingly, a hen harrier. House martins, swallows and swifts come here in the summer to skim and sip the water, leaving tiny trails on the surface which disappear almost instantly, ephemeral as a musical note. In the surrounding reeds and gorse there are redstarts, yellowhammers, wheatears, flycatchers. From March to July every sound is accompanied by the trill of skylarks, occasionally punctuated by the trailing calls of curlews carrying from the nearby fields.

Today, as I approach the pool from the summit of the hill, I see no birds at all. The anxiety increases. I have nightmares about this place, about the day when the long draining down of wild things becomes complete. On days like today I get glimpses of it. I head for the big oak which stands next to the reeds. It is still holding on to its leaves, which are patched and veined with bronze. Across the water a stand of Scots pines are looking sickly. Behind them an old thorn tree stands skeletal between the water and a hollowed-out barrow. The place has a funerary feel, common at this time of year, but I feel it more keenly today, which is the last day of the COP26 climate change conference. For almost two weeks I've been following developments at the event, which has been promoted as our last, last chance to keep global temperature rises below 1.5 degrees Celsius. Once again it seems that the corporations and fossil-fuel lobbyists have got the kind of agreement that will keep them in business for decades. Once again Western politicians have taken the stage and made their promises while simultaneously ordering their negotiators in back rooms to break them. We are heading into a world that will be at least partially uninhabitable. I don't know how easy it is for the people of these islands to imagine what an inhospitable place looks like. I think it looks like this: broken trees, bare, cratered ground, flat water mirroring a birdless sky. Stone silence.

I cross the stream that feeds the pool. Sometimes there are snipe here, hidden in the bracken. Today there are none. I walk around the edge, watching the water's surface change and change again, dark as a bruise, light as the white of an eye. It is almost totally silent, the only sound the faint hiss of reeds and slap of wavelets hitting the bank. My ears focus on the inward sounds of my heartbeat, the high-pitched whistling of tinnitus like a bird call stretched to infinity. And then I hear the rippling of wings and notice that the row of hawthorns that lines the far edge of the pool is filled with little silhouettes, camouflaged inside tangled twigs and branches. They flee from me now, flowing from tree to tree. They are fieldfares, recently arrived from Scandinavia. They rush away noisily and flee to a high bank above the water, waiting for me to pass. I sigh happily and speak clumsy words of greeting to the Norse raiders. The world has come back to life. Another dawn has arrived.

*

The river is brown and cloudy, moving fast. It has risen a metre or more overnight and is now lapping at the edge of the nearby town. People are moving their cars, knowing that the last time the water rose this fast several were washed downstream, ending up perched in trees or half-buried in gravel and mud. I'm on the bridge, watching the flood. The railings on either side have rusted out in places and become dangerous. They are guarded by temporary fences. I'm staring through the bars and getting that strange sensation that sometimes comes to me in high places, the dark urge to lean out further. A few minutes ago I pulled my car to the side of the road to let a fire engine pass. It was towing a lifeboat. Someone is in the river.

The trees on the banks are still in leaf, soaking up the fading glow of the day like huge, black sponges. By dawn the banks will have burst and the water will spread north turning the fields into a lake a mile wide and five miles long, cut into sections by drowned hedges. In the middle of it will be an old brick cottage, abandoned now, uninhabitable due to repeated flooding. I visit the place sometimes, walking in through the front entrance, the old door hanging from one hinge, the living-room walls showing the mould-green line marking the height of the last flood.

When I was a boy I was terrified of still water. I had repeated nightmares where I was standing in a derelict building, next to a swimming pool covered with slime and weed. A slow wave appeared, caressing the full length of the pool then rebounding back as if some huge creature were doing lengths in the depths. A mile or so from my house there was a canal that bordered the edge of the colliery before cutting into the heart of the city. It was in poor repair at the time. The water was slicked, stagnant and opaque. Rotting boats were moored alongside it and there were deep, black-walled locks. Floating in one was the body of a dead dog. There were other still waters. The city was pockmarked with abandoned industrial sites that had been partially cleared and were reverting to scrub with little pools and sad, coppery streams that ran into culverts, protected with rusted gates. The remains of demolished mills could be identified by shallow ponds surrounded by scrubby, sick-looking trees. Slag heaps leached their run-offs into ditches and streams, tributaries of the River Trent, which collected the poisons and poured them out, eventually into the North Sea.

A short distance from my parents' house was a pond that had been part of a dyeing mill until the end of the nineteenth century. The pond was shallow and infested with a thick algae that stank for most of the summer. In the winter, as the algae rotted down, iridescent slicks spread across the water. Many of the trees that bordered the pond had toppled and lay on their sides in the shallows. I imagined the place to be full of underwater traps: broken glass, rusted wire. Even the tiny fish that crowded the shallows were covered in spines. A friend of mine, almost as a joke, spent an afternoon fishing in the pool. Each time he cast and reeled back a green tassel of weed was attached to his line. I stood next to him as he cast as far as he could into the centre of the pond and as he began to reel it back something snatched the line. The rod bent over in a tight arc and he had trouble holding on to it. As he leaned back against the pull something mirror-bright broke the surface of the water and rolled. The rod continued to bend as the huge fish thrashed, cutting up the water and sending wide rings out to the pond's edges. Then the line snapped, the rod twanged back and the monster disappeared. The water gradually smoothed as we stood in shock. The story spread about the great pike and for months afterwards local fishermen came and tried their skills, but it was never caught. After that experience the pond became a bigger source of fear for me. I imagined that beneath its still surface it was miles deep, connected to underground shafts that passed through the mines and stretched all the way to the sea, filled with lurking, scaly creatures. It was a place of darkness in the daytime, poisoned, but fiercely wild.

A young woman is crossing the bridge at dusk on a mid-winter evening. The woman is bent a little, wrapping a wool coat tightly around her, tucking her head into the collar. One hand is in her pocket, the other holds a rope attached to the head collar of a pony, which is also bent, its head sagging from its ewe neck. They are struggling against the wind, which carries swirls of snow, the sky starting to fill, flakes catching the last light and holding on to it as they fall. She turns to look as the snow drifts below the rails on the bridge, down to the surface of the river where they dissolve in the dark water. It is the last time she'll see the river. She has miles to go, over two high hills to her home. Two hours later, wet and freezing, she will pass the summit of the first hill. Later, at its foot, she will cross the little River Bachawy, a tributary of the Wye. She will struggle halfway up the next hill. At the peak of the storm, her pony will stumble, she will fall and break her ankle. She will lie in the knee-deep snow unable to move, and she will die only a few miles from her home where her six small children are waiting for her. A stone monument is set in the place where she died. She is known as the Martyr of the Storm.

The story haunts me. The thought of six children peering out at the blizzard while their mother lies dying, and the precarity of life only an instant before the machine age arrived with technologies that would shield the community from storms of all kinds. I'm also haunted by the image of her crossing the river, away from the safety of the town where she was offered shelter, deciding to bend into the storm instead. The river was a different place then, abundant, diverse. While the woman struggled with the elements the inhabitants of the river slept, oblivious to the storm, which was only a thing made of air.

I'm standing near the place where the woman made her decision to risk the storm. The sun has dipped below the horizon where the river turns north. For years I've been coming to this spot to watch the water and its winged and finned inhabitants. Sometimes there are egrets here, high priests of the shallows, blazing pure white, making their grey cousins the herons look like bowed and impoverished preachers. In the summer I can lean out and see the bronze shades of chub using the stone pillars to shelter from the current. There are the swifts hurtling upstream and downstream, close enough for me to hear the rush of their wings.

I used to think that life stretched out endlessly, like an ocean. Then I got to know about limits, about death, about sickness, how suddenly it can come, how relentless it is, how helpless we can be even with our technologies. For me, coming to the bridge to watch this ancient river be transformed by the four-billion-year-old dusk is an act of gratitude, for the beauty that remains in spite of everything.

*

I've been up all night listening to the hissing edge of the sea. Later in the day I'll board a plane and say goodbye to Kenya, and to the vast land of Africa. After a year-long journey I'm about to go home. A pale line has spread across the sky creating a graduation of deep red against the indigo. I can just see the faint outlines of clouds and the hard edge of the reef wall a mile away. A minute more and I can make out the pale edges of the waves breaking against it. I hear the first bird call, a high shriek I cannot identify. As it sounds, a warm breeze strokes my skin.

I stand up, take off my shirt, pull on my goggles and walk into the water. A thin blanket of clinging weed gathers around my feet and for a second I think about retreating. Then I wade out and swim. I stroke slowly, keeping my head above the surface, breathing easily, watching the water ripple out from my arms. The tropical sea is at body temperature and I seem part of it, as if the edges of me have dissolved. I keep up the same slow stroke, no current to swim against in this slackest of tides.

There is enough light now to look at the bottom: smooth white sand, round stones, horse tails of green weed. Just ahead of me is a school of tiny silver fish, little splinters. They twitch and disappear. A few minutes later I swim over the edge of the reef, a little cliff which rises to meet me, and I see the first of its outgrowths, a smooth, mushroom-shaped plinth, which is shadowless, bathed in a blue twilight. At its base is a group of sea urchins, their black spines entangled. A lionfish hovers above them, its fins ruffling like tattered prayer flags. Soon the water is glowing with the clean light of dawn and the myriad colours of the reef are appearing, colours I will never see again. So many impossible forms: bone trees, watery flowers, feathered stones. I swim through luminous schools of fish, fish with stripes, with spots and daubs, with beaks, trumpet mouths, with streamer tails and swallow tails. Some are translucent, others transparent, some generate their own light. There are fish that speed through the spaces between the reef's outgrowths, others that move ponderously, their tails tacking slowly. Some suspend themselves vertically and hang like skinny lanterns. There are thousands of species in this section of a reef which extends for over 150 miles, a seascape that shimmers with life. Their names are strange and beautiful: triggerfish, needlefish, surgeonfish, threadfish, bleny, glassy, sardinella, frogfish. Their features are a fantasy, starry, false-eyed, gold-silked, powder-blued, double-banded, glow-bellied. In the shallows of this place are dugongs and spinner dolphins. In its deeps are coelacanths, fish that have been swimming Earth's oceans for four hundred million years.

I swim slowly through this submerged paradise, diving down between the narrow ravines of the reef, among startled and unconcerned creatures of every shape, their colours stained with a lobster-blue wash. I can hear the rush of water, muffled and amplified. There are other sounds at the edge of my hearing that I cannot make out, little chirpings, rapid ticks, pulses and knocks, low groans and creaks. I lift my head and look around to see if fishermen are working nearby, but there are no boats. I drift in the almost-still sea, holding my arms out, trying not to move so that I can hear more clearly. The strange noises come in waves, build and subside. Perhaps it's the sound of the reef shifting under the weight of the tide, or water running through tubes and channels, the tapping of loose stones. Satisfied with this explanation I turn and begin to swim back to the beach. Time to go home.

Acropora millepora is a coral species widespread in the Indian and Pacific oceans, particularly on shallow reefs. The colony creates an irregular cushion made up of dense clusters of small, treelike forms. It is one of the most colourful corals. Some are deep green, some salmon pink, some deep purple or jade blue. All have an almost neon luminosity. The polyps are tube-like at the tip of each branch with a radial assemblage beneath. These radials are shaped like protruding lower lips. They grow slowly, no more than ten centimetres per year. As one of the most common coral species on the Kenyan reef their aragonite skeletons make up a large proportion of the reef shelf, a building process which has taken millennia.

Seven years after my dawn swim, the water temperatures above the reef reached unprecedented highs during a period when El Niño combined with unusual atmospheric conditions. A mass bleaching event ensued which wiped out almost 80 per cent of soft corals and reduced overall species numbers by 50 per cent. The kaleidoscopic underwater garden turned into a place of bones in just a few months. *Acropora millepora,* which is more sensitive to temperature fluctuations than most larger corals, was one of the major casualties, dying back in huge numbers. Only 10 per cent survived.

Within a year algal growth increased significantly and large numbers of herbivorous fish began to invade. The ecology of the reef was transformed. Since then the decline has continued, partly due to the outpouring of sediment and chemicals from the country's rivers, which are being silted up with run-off from increasingly industrialised agriculture. More recently sand harvesting for construction projects on the shallow reef shelf has also become a problem. Dredgers up to 150 metres long and capable of holding 20,000 tons work the coastal shelf stirring up huge clouds of sand which are then carried by the tide on to the reef. Only small areas of the reef remain wholly intact, places where cool currents have kept the sea temperatures down.

I've often thought of going back to the place where I swam that morning. The beach would be unchanged I'm sure, the buildings overlooking it, mostly hotels, mostly occupied by wealthy Westerners, would be pristine. The sun would float up from the ocean beautifully, projecting mesmerising colours into the sky. But as I slid beneath the surface of the water the rainbow garden I vividly remember would be gone.

*

The ocean is mostly a place of darkness. Even where sunlight penetrates a blue fog always hangs, sometimes thick as soup, at others a dawn haze blurring out details. Most objects are a hint or a shadow. Sight is the least reliable of senses underwater. We've recorded a quarter of a million oceanic species, but there are possibly ten times that number we've never seen. We can, however, continue our exploration by listening.

The muscles which surround the swim bladders of most bony fish are adapted to create sound as well as buoyancy. They contract and convulse to pop, squeak, groan and even roar. Other species use spinelike protrusions to knock and tap. In large reef systems the combination of these sounds creates a strange percussive symphony, as loud as road traffic.

In the ocean there are dawn and dusk choruses just as on land. At dawn night feeders quieten and the fish that hunt in daylight start to call. At dusk the process reverses. This phenomenon occurs in every sea and ocean. We're familiar with the clicking of dolphins and the deep moans of whales, but we have little knowledge of the rest of the marine soundscape. Recordings are made by dropping hydrophones from boats, islands or floating platforms, making it difficult to locate the source of the sounds as we can't visually identify them. Nevertheless these sounds are being increasingly documented.

I'm listening through headphones to the dawn chorus off Port Hedland in Western Australia, an area where recordings have been made over several years. These are the mingled calls of snapping shrimps, croakers, terapontids, batfish. There are hoots and burbles, buzzes, trumpets, growls. Some of the sounds could almost be terrestrial, the snuffle of a bear, grunt of a wild boar, snort of a leopard, screech of an owl or coo of a dove. But they're often strangely unnatural, some utterly alien, as if synthesised by a machine. The chorus fluctuates over a twenty-four-hour period and the wider soundscape changes according to season, water temperature and even lunar cycles. In shallower waters most day-active fish are brightly coloured or patterned, their visual faculty still prominent. Their quieter calls are drowned out at dusk by the chorus of night feeders whose sonic world is far more intense.

Sound travels at approximately 1,500 metres per second

through water, around five times its speed through air. Its direction of travel is dictated by temperature and pressure. As temperature lowers sound refracts downwards. In very deep areas of the ocean the temperature becomes constant, but pressure increases, making sound refract upwards. In the middle of the twentieth century an American and a Russian scientist simultaneously discovered the existence of a deep-water sound channel at approximately one kilometre below the surface which, due to its constant pressure and temperature, acts as a waveguide, a mechanism which allows sound to travel with little dissipation. In this band of water low-frequency sounds can travel thousands of miles. Many applications were trialled for the channel, including submarine detection, military warning systems and the monitoring of volcanic activity. Some whales deliberately dive to visit the channel in order to communicate across distances. We humans identify pods of whales visually, watching them breach in small groups. But individuals in their communities may be hundreds of miles apart, communicating with the group via the sound channel.

A sperm whale creates sound in the tubular structures of its head, clicks and moans that vibrate at different pitches and tempos. These codas are spoken slightly differently by each whale and are used to identify individuals, acting effectively as a name. They develop in juveniles in a similar way to a human child learning to speak, beginning with uncontrolled babbling sounds which later develop into click patterns which match the dialect of the clan. Humpback whales continually transform their dialects and their songs, a process which is little understood. It was thought that clans picked up the songs of other clans through a process of learning similar to humans, but recent studies indicate that some sound patterns are emitted by individuals who have never been in contact with the group they were thought to be imitating. The whales have a level of sophistication that allows them to continuously develop and change languages rapidly, several times each decade, creating codas which overlap and echo those created by other, distant communities, while still being able to understand each other. The speech of whales could be far more developed than that of human beings, a skill which has been honed by the deep twilight of the oceans over millions of years.

Oceans contain 99.5 per cent of all the inhabitable space on Earth. We land dwellers use only a speck of the available space on the planet. The greatest migratory movement of species happens in the world's deep oceans every day, twice a day. Dawn and dusk are vertical phenomena for all sea creatures, an upwelling or downwelling of light. Trillions of marine creatures move in response to this daily phenomenon, either coming up from the half-light or permanent midnight of the deep, or moving down away from dark-dwelling predators. In terms of biomass this migration dwarfs the better-known seasonal migrations of birds, or the movements of grazing mammals across the great plains. So many creatures are on the move that some ships' captains have observed their depth gauges and thought that their vessels were about to run aground, though they were travelling through seas miles deep. As the fish and invertebrates come up towards the surface they seek other species to prey on while attempting to conceal themselves from their own predators. The easiest way for prey to be identified is from below, where their silhouettes can be seen against the field of light above them. This field is ever-changing as they rise and sunlight fades. They use a form of bioluminescence to combat this, a method known as counter-illumination.

Bioluminescent cells occur in almost 80 per cent of sea species. Though some lights are used as lures, seeing aids or alarm flashes, the cells are usually concentrated in patches and appendages located mainly on a creature's undersides for the purpose of counter-illumination. Many methods have evolved for the production of this bioluminescence. Some fish have evolved photophores which employ concave mirrors, while others use lenses or fibre optics. They are able to filter the light produced so that the colours match those of the surrounding water. These methods are energy intensive, taking a toll on the creature to produce, particularly as they get closer to the surface where the vast majority of food exists, and also the brightest solar light. The daily migration to and from the surface is a journey taken at great risk, requiring the constant, perfect adjustment of emitted luminescence against the surrounding atmospheric light. Given the huge numbers of animals moving together, mistakes are almost always fatal.

Evolutionary adaptations in some of the predators dwelling in the twilight of the oceans are remarkable. There are fish which hang vertically to create the smallest possible silhouette while watching with huge eyes for the shapes of prey above them, springing upwards like thrown spears to catch them. Others hunt in the pitch dark of the midnight zone as well as in the light. Many of these species have asymmetrical eyes, one pointing up and the other down. The upwards eye is much bigger than the downwards, which needs only to identify sparks in the depths. Perhaps the most extraordinary of all adaptations is in barreleyes, or spook fish, which carry rotating lenses inside perfectly transparent heads like mini observatories.

For a person to witness the daily twilight migration in the ocean, suspended at, say, a hundred metres deep, would be like watching dusk rise, not fall, as if in a well or lift shaft, a vertical graduation of light to dark carrying a swarm of life so dense that it clouds the solar light as it rises. Below a world of sparks and flashes would appear, tail lights, lighthouse beams, spewed clouds and wakes of colour.

*

At St David's Head cowslips, stonecrop, thrift and sea campions grow in profusion among the rocks and on the cliff ledges. They nod and flutter in the wind, which is dying as the still point of twilight nears. The gulls have sensed it. They fly out into the bay towards Skomer, tethered to each other with an invisible line, as if tied to the vanished sun. The sea is running south, funnelled through Ramsey and Jack sounds, which churn up the fast-moving water. There are falls and steps, eddies and races. In the last light the writhing surface carries a predatory menace and, simultaneously, a

sense of stillness coming from the depths beneath, though all of it is on the move, rising towards the glow.

I come to this area often, camping in the fields near to the cliffs. I catch the boat over to Skomer, or kayak beneath the cave-pierced cliffs, sliding over the clear water and the blue boulders. Once I paddled towards two grey seals sprawled on a rock at the entrance to a high cave. There was a flock of choughs skipping over the cliff wall, their piercing calls echoing. Then a peregrine appeared high up, diving towards one of the choughs at full speed, its wings tucked into its sides. In the last second the chough lurched sideways and the peregrine missed its target. It opened its wings, arced and climbed back to where it had come from, where it looped and screeched and plummeted again, this time with no target in mind, just for the rush of it. The choughs were gone. The seals hadn't noticed, or if they had, this was an occurrence so common to them that it didn't require attention. The peregrine disappeared into the sting of its call. It was the highlight of a year of lockdowns, the only time I got to the sea that summer, the only time I managed to take part in the wildness of things. I've since spent many twilights here, sitting on a cliff edge where the world still seems immense and teeming with life. Bird populations in this area are thriving at the moment. Even the curlew is hanging on, still nesting in the area, though it has disappeared almost everywhere else in Wales. I hear them often, crossing the sounds between the mainland and the islands. When I come here I fall in love again. The list of species which pass through the spaces between the islands and the mainland each year is huge. The paths they follow lead everywhere, from the

Arctic to Antarctic, into Africa, across Eurasia and the Americas. If we're going to finally learn how to live as part of a community which includes the wild perhaps we should start in a place like this, educate ourselves with what lives and breathes around us, and send out the evangelists like St David did fifteen hundred years ago. Let's educate hearts first, minds will follow.

Two visitors row back from Skomer at dusk, attempting to cross Jack Sound in their wooden boat while the tide is slack. Clouds are gathering on the horizon, the wind starting to shave the tops of the waves. As the swell builds their progress slows and when they eventually move out past the lee of the island the tide race through the sound is in full flow, pushing them north, away from the sheltered cove they are steering for and out into the open sea. They take turns to row and make no progress as the wind continues to build and the waves start to break over the sides of the boat. Night has now almost descended, the line of the cliffs fading, their landmarks the lit windows of cottages on the headland. Soon the storm moves over them and rain comes down so hard it obscures the view of land completely. They are travelling blind, heading north with the tide, hoping they are not being pushed towards the cliffs on the opposite side of the bay. One man rows, the other bails. The waves build higher and the men fight for their lives, the boat coming close to capsizing over and over again.

After hours of rowing and with the sea still building the boat nears a stack and the men feel the swell lessen a little as the waves break against the rock. They fight to keep the boat in this patch of water and for the rest of the night they manage to stay close to the stack without being smashed against it. As dawn approaches the storm begins to ease, the wind and waves calming. When the first stain of sunlight picks out the cliffs they turn and row for the bay. A few hours later, aided by the now south-flowing tide, they beach the boat at Broad Haven and walk home.

This event happened in the 1950s when Skomer was still being farmed and transport to and from the island was undertaken mainly by rowing boat, even to carry livestock and crops. Occasional storms were hazards the community had to endure and sometimes there were fatalities. Shortly afterwards the farm was abandoned and the island became a wildlife reserve. This period marked the beginning of the great acceleration, when seas began the warming that continues at an ever-greater speed.

There are few boats sunk in Jack Sound these days, but the storms that come out of the Atlantic Ocean are now more frequent and intense. Though currently thriving, seabird colonies are under threat from these storms. Inshore birds like shags and cormorants, which shelter from predators on cliffs at night, can be washed away and drowned by waves. Overwintering pelagic birds like puffins, guillemots, razorbills and kittiwakes are under greater threat. Though they can weather storms easily the fish they feed on are driven much deeper to avoid rough water, therefore moving beyond the reach of birds which dive to feed. Starvation follows. After the storm-wracked winter of 2014, tens of thousands of seabirds were washed up dead on the beaches of Wales, Cornwall, the Channel Islands, Brittany and northern Spain.

Hundreds of thousands more died without trace, jeopardising island colonies.

Atlantic puffins are perhaps the most loveable of all seabirds. They are stunning to look at in their breeding colours, with large, bright scarlet and sulphur striped beaks, plump black and white torsos and red legs. Their scurrying, scuttling, purring activities near to their nests attract huge attention from wildlife lovers and they have become the main draw to the Pembrokeshire islands. On Skomer there are over 25,000 breeding birds, their numbers increasing since surveys began. But globally the number of Atlantic puffins is in freefall and they are now classed as vulnerable to extinction. The population is projected to decline by up to 70 per cent by mid-century, the main cause being starvation due to overfishing and winter storms. The cliffs of Skomer may become more dense with the remnant population if shoals of sand eels, on which they depend, continue to thrive in nearby waters. But this is a coin toss. It is as likely that the island will gradually become deserted. The great swarm of life in summer will be reduced exponentially. After its brief rewilding, we will have tamed the island again.

*

The River Wye is a presence that dominates this part of the valley more than any other, more than the giant whalebacks of the mountains, the scrawled rectangles of the fields or the twisted monuments of the ancient oaks. More even than the little town with its history filled with princes, nobles, vagabonds, thieves, lovers and murderers. The river is the place everything returns to, fragmented and dissolved. Everyone knows something about it: the view from the bridge when the ice that had covered the river for weeks broke up in an instant and floated downstream in long, saw-toothed shards which jostled, collided and chimed like dull bells; or the great salmon that have been landed, record catches, of which most of us have only seen faded photographs and handwritten records; or the tragic drownings when the river boiled.

Once I saw an otter, just once, out in the middle of the river, swimming in tight circles, chasing and catching its tail, and I cried because it entered my world only a few days after I'd visited a house high on the hill which was filled with the stuffed heads of the wild things of the valley. The old man who lived there told me about his best day out hunting, back in the decade I was born, when he killed three otters in a morning, and let the next one go, considering it unsporting to take four in a day. As he was talking his nonagenerian body was shaking with excitement, the connection still live to his old lust.

In a field adjoining the old man's house is a little spring, the beginning of a narrow stream, a thread in the grass, which trickles down the hill to join a broader stream running through the village, under the road and on to the Wye. These threads of water are used by otters to find their way up to the hill common, following their secret routes through steep ravines and dense copses. The hunting range of an otter is roughly twenty square miles. Within that territory the creature knows in great detail every twist in the river. It knows which stream to follow from the Wye to the high pool in the first week of April, when toads come to spawn in their thousands. It knows where trout rest in the summer, every stony weir and waterfall when the salmon are running, every hiding place and potential holt. There is so much to learn in its decade-long life.

I've lived in this place for twice the lifespan of an otter and I feel I've learned so little of the terrain. I can reel off a compact history of the area, name some of its more dignified inhabitants and talk a little about the culture that has transformed it into what it is now. But it's knowledge that focuses only on my own species and its preoccupations. The otter is an inhabitant. We are occupants. The word inhabit means to dwell in, to hold on to, to give to or receive. To occupy is to seize, to possess. The castles and ruined fortifications, the huge factory farms, the dams, mines and quarries which litter Wales are proof of the long occupation we are still undertaking.

The image of the river I will always carry inside me is the upstream view from the bridge. It runs in a wide channel between overhanging trees, a boulevard of water. In any weather and at any time of year it is a picture-postcard scene, the water quivering from pewter to silver. Visitors always take a picture here, standing at the centre on the bridge, capturing the always-different, always-the-same image. Our lives intersect here, our rivers of story stretching into the distance, taking a thousand meandering routes. They reach upstream into the invisibility of tomorrow, and downstream into the dawn of our culture. But the river itself is cut away when the shutter comes down. Unlike the inhabitants of the place, we occupiers do not navigate by it, or recognise our dependence on it. It's a glimpse for us on our routes elsewhere, a brief illumination like a glimmer of red at sunset, soon forgotten, eclipsed by the next place, the next task or target.

The River Llynfi is a small tributary of the Wye, not much wider than a stream, threading through rolling country from its source at Llangorse Lake to where it meets the Wye just above Glasbury, a favourite swimming place for locals. In the summer of 2020, there was a pollution spill there, probably from a bordering farm, and the inhabitants of the river were wiped out by poisoned water. Many tens of thousands of fish died as well as huge numbers of invertebrates. When the poisoning was reported by residents who lived near the river, inspectors took too long to reach the place where the spill had happened. By the time they arrived the poison had washed downstream and no one was ever held accountable. The Llynfi had been poisoned before, a decade previously, and had only just recovered its biodiversity after major work by volunteers. It was estimated that the pollution was only present for one hour. It took ten years for the river to come to life, an hour for it to die.

After the event attention was drawn to the wider Wye catchment and the intensive farming practices that have taken hold here, particularly the production of poultry. Hangar-like sheds have been built on farms all along the Wye Valley where eggs and meat are produced in huge quantities. Most of the waste from these units is spread on to nearby land and is washed into the river, raising the levels of phosphates, causing algal blooms which blanket the lower reaches of the river, wiping out aquatic plants due to the blocking of light. Step into the river on a late summer's day and your feet slip on the slime that coats the stony bottom. Swim in it and you can smell the toilet odour of the water. Dive down into it and you enter a green smog. You can feel the river suffocating in the man-made half-light.

*

I'm staring up at a cloudless sky along receding lines of larch trunks. The wood grows on the slopes of a high-sided valley and even on a day as bright as this, the place is shadowed. The only sign of the sun's presence is in the crowns of the larches, which blaze like fireworks. Lower down the slope are beech trees and sweet chestnuts, half skeletal now but retaining gold and tangerine in their last leaves. In the wood is a famous waterfall, a place people have been visiting for hundreds of years, with the fabulous name of Water-Break-its-Neck. This place was once heathland, but in the Victorian era the landowners decided to enhance its beauty by planting an array of trees, many of them exotic species, grown from seeds taken from distant continents. Many thrived. Among the larches there are towering western cedars and sequoias, their trunks funnelling out of the earth like volcanoes.

The place is busy, no spaces in the car park, groups of people heading up and down the maze of paths that wind through the wood to and from the falls. I follow the signs and find myself on a rolling route that twists by the side of a shallow stream. The ravine narrows as the path progresses, and the air is filled with moisture. The cliffs on either side are thick with ferns and saxifrages. Twisted trees cling to the rocks, their twigs and branches so draped with bearded moss that no bark is visible. The exposed mudstone is fractured and thinly layered and the high waterfall sheets over these layers and slides into a pool below. The combination of its soft, hypnotic sound and the emerald twilight it is bathed in could lull an insomniac to sleep. The place is Tolkien-esque, Rackham-esque, a fairy wood. There is a woman sitting cross-legged on a boulder only a few metres from the falls. She is utterly still, her eyes shut, breathing deeply. I keep back from the water so as not to disturb her. Within a minute a family arrives with two youngsters intent on wading into the stream and touching the falling water. Their parents are calling out to them. Another family arrives with multiple dogs and the meditator's peace is shattered.

On a log which is tilted into the stream I notice rows of coins sticking out from cracks in the dead wood. Next to the log, placed among the layers of the mudstone cliff, are stones which have been scratched with names, messages, roughly engraved love hearts, kisses. There are hundreds of them. The woman now stands up looking a little dazed. She peers along the path at three more approaching families. It will be a while before she manages to meditate again.

In this twilit space that echoes with the sound of the falls there is an elsewhere that is almost touchable. Children, every one a little animist, are born with a sense of mystery in nature, though we educate it out of them. It returns at times, in places like this. The woman, I'm sure, was talking to the water. Others have left little messages on the stones that could be seen by some cultures as acts of worship, offerings to the gods of tree, rock and water. I walk back to the car park. Next to the gate is a little sign, stapled to a stake leaning out of the ground. At the top of it, in bold letters, is the message 'Trees are dying'.

I'm watching a video recording showing a species of water mould called *Phytophthora ramorum*, filmed through a microscope lens. A sporangium is floating in clear liquid like the flattened head of a flower cast into a pool. Around it dozens of little zoospores are somehow propelling themselves backwards and forwards, zipping in and out of view. The sporangium contains a mass of spores and begins to pulse and squeeze itself until it spits out a cluster. Once released the spores separate, accelerate and disappear from view while others form to replace them. In the short sequence of a few minutes the sporangium releases masses of them. This pathogenic process is rapid and relentless enough to attack even the largest and most ancient trees across a host of species. Symptoms begin with the partial blackening of leaves and progress to the formation of bleeding wounds on branches before internal processes stop working and the tree dies. Larch and oak trees are particularly susceptible. The water mould is carried in streams and ponds, in rain droplets and water vapour. A narrow ravine with a waterfall running through it is the perfect place for it to thrive.

The fairy tale wood is dying. Over the coming years some of the trees will topple or be cut down and burned in an attempt to limit the spread of the disease. The stream running from the waterfall will carry spores for miles as it joins the little River Arrow, a tributary of the Lugg, which joins the Wye in one of the most wooded landscapes in Britain. In a twenty-year period from its initial discovery in a single plant from a garden centre in Sussex ramorum disease has spread across hundreds of thousands of hectares, thriving in the watery landscapes and wet weather conditions. There is no cure.

*

I'm driving through hills I should know but don't. I've never been this way before. This part of Wales, home to the huge sheep ranches of Radnorshire, has always seemed desolate to me, more scraped back than anywhere else I know. But now I'm looking for the source of a little river I've stood beside further downstream for hours each November, waiting for a glimpse of a salmon. The Edw is possibly the most beautiful and the most secret tributary of the Wye. It tumbles twenty miles through hidden valleys from the eastern edge of the Cambrian Mountains, never much wider than a stream.

It is a day at the end of the year, after weeks of dark, when the land has been draped in thick cloud, the sun only appearing occasionally to spear through and illuminate one of the gloomiest months I've ever known. But in the past hour the clouds have broken and there are patches of blue up there, though the sun is just below the horizon. I turn on to a narrow lane and park where a gate marks the beginning of a common. Beyond it are sheep in their hundreds, boggy ground, tufts of sedge, and a thin line of water where the Edw runs through a shallow ditch choked with gorse and bracken. It is a few centimetres deep and narrow enough to step across.

When my boys were little they used to follow streams like this to their sources high on the hill. For the boys it was an adventure; they chased the threads of water through woods and narrow ravines, up on to the common, until they were breathless, then splashed in the bright green soak where water bubbled clear from the ground, churning it to mud with their little feet. Before they were born I followed similar streams around a little town in the middle of the Algerian Desert, wondering how these threads of coolness were even possible in such a hot and hostile place. I marvelled at the little silver glimmers that flashed below the surface, wondering what species of fish could survive in the Sahara, kneeling at the edge of the water, repeating over and over the beautiful name of the place: Timimoun, *Ti-mi-moun*. Later I was in Jinja, Uganda, bordering the vast, freshwater sea of Lake Victoria, where the Nile flows out of it, the disputed, and utterly arbitrary, source of the great river. We have an obsession with the beginning and end points of things. The discovery of the Nile's source was a colonial misadventure, taking decades, costing many lives, twisting ancient territories out of shape, to feed the imaginations of Victorians. But all rivers have multiple sources, they do not follow a single thread from start to finish. They're shaped like vines, tendrils reaching in every direction.

I've already given up on the idea of finding the source of the Edw. I can see so many tracks where water has cut down the hill into the stream. And I've chanced on something far more interesting. On the way here I've seen little flocks of starlings scissoring across the road, moving fast as if trying to meet a deadline. They were all heading to this place. What I originally thought, when I stepped out of the car, was the chattering sound of the stream is actually a hundred thousand birds calling to each other. The pine plantation that borders the stream is a major winter roost site. It is alive with sound. Starlings are arriving from every direction. The flocks undulate with the terrain, then rise steeply and circle over the trees. A dark band appears, thrown grain against the horizon, and as quickly disappears into the camouflage of the trees. Then, for a few seconds, a mass of birds rise, smoke flowing against the wind. They spread rapidly, flooding the sky. They transmogrify, their shapes no longer avian but riverine. The flock moves in ripples and waves, eddies and backflows. It breaks, sprays out and crashes in on itself. The sound continues to build like rising water engulfing the surrounding space. More birds arrive in little tributaries. The spectacle grows as the light fades. At nautical twilight, the flying ceases. What remains is the blanket shadow of the trees, congealing cloud, points of starlight appearing in the gaps. The birds continue to call noisily until the sky goes completely dark, when gradually the sound fades and what is left is the little hushing stream of the Edw and the occasional hiss of tyres from the distant road.

The plantation that the birds roost in is surrounded by five snow-white structures which tower above it like giant watchers. Each has three huge arms spread out as if signalling to a distant audience, giving directions or perhaps warning. The arms do not move, even in this wind which bends and whips the sedge at my feet. The wind farm is not yet online. The turbines stand still, immaculate and new, yet somehow they give off the atmosphere of old monuments, as if something of their scale could only have been made when the hills themselves were shaped. They will go live in the next few months. This is the last winter that the murmuration will happen undisturbed by them. Next year they will be turning in the wind, and as the tributaries of the flock arrive from every direction there will be blades crossing their path. Starlings are known for roosting in and around man-made structures, the most spectacular winter murmuration in the country happening at the derelict pier in Brighton, but it's not known if moving structures like wind turbines displace flocks. This winter could possibly be the peak for this spectacle. I'm going to be here for as many dusks as I can manage in the next few weeks, standing by the narrow headwater of the Edw, where the salmon spawn just downstream, watching the river of birds.

*

For days it has rained heavily and the river is swollen again. Roads are flooded, some villages cut off. I'm standing just downstream of the bridge, watching the sky fade beyond it. The trees that fringe the water are scribbled jet black, silhouetted like the man who is now crossing the bridge following his dog, their simple shapes tiny above the river, which is huge and boiling. Its surface is so multiply riven, so animated and tangled, it's impossible to take in. Out in the middle the water snakes and plumes, rides its own undercurrents and rips. At its edge it smooths into pools which slowly turn in the stream then begin to boil up as if something beneath is sucking and blowing. A kingfisher flees just above my head, little water bee, colourless now against the last glow of the sky. A blackbird is calling from the bushes behind me, a single note on rapid repeat. I don't know if the birds are as shaken as I am, looking at this river, the power of it, its unknowableness. Its multiple forms mock our limitations. I can't think of any poet who has come near to capturing this, any painter. Perhaps music works best. The recent work of John Luther Adams expresses oceanic movement, the rush of huge volumes of water, the blending of currents and cross-currents. Its space and depth, its thunder. But perhaps not the relentlessness, the otherness, the huge complexity we will never be able to fathom.

It's our fate on this ocean-facing island, if our direction of travel as a culture continues, to face the rising waters, the ever-more-frequently boiling rivers. We may continue to poison them, to carve, block and silt them up for a time yet, believing as we do that they are simply our resources to be harnessed. But they will outlast us and their waters will run clean, eventually. There will come a time when this stretch of river will flow wilder than it does now. The bridge will be elsewhere, repurposed. Its huge concrete pillars, which look as though they can withstand every future deluge, will eventually be splintered, atomised to mossy boulders, smooth pebbles, skimming stones. Everything we make dissolves in time. The proof is to be found in the graveyard of the little church high on the hill. There are many blank headstones, the names and dedications that were carved into them only a few centuries ago now smoothed away, eroded by the caress of rain. As each drop landed and ran off, it took with it a grain of stone, the fragment of a name, which it carried back to the streams, to become part of the silt below the gravel, the place where salmon return from the ocean to spawn.

WHO SPEAKS FOR WOLF?

It is a story that has been passed down for generations among the Iroquois. It begins when the people need to find new land to support their growing numbers. They send out scouts to look for a new place in the forest, one which can provide fertile soil for their crops, good hunting, timber for building and access to clear water. Among the people was a man they called Wolf Brother, because he knew the ways of the wolves and was able to befriend them, to mimic their calls and be part of their hunt. When scouts returned to report on the new lands Wolf Brother was not present and a decision was made without him as to where the new village would be. When the time came the people moved to their new land and they built longhouses and planted crops in the forest. They caught deer and squirrel and had access to springs and streams. In the winter they had shelter from the winds and plenty of fuel. But sometimes when meat was hung out to cure it would be gone the next day. This happened more and more. Then they found that the wolves had become bold and had started to roam among their houses at night. At first they made provision for this and left food for the wolves at the edge of the village. But the wolves came more. Eventually they had no choice but to send people to keep watch around the perimeter and to scare the wolves away when they came. But there were too many wolves and more and more people were needed, so many that they didn't have the time or energy to plant crops or to hunt. In the end they had to make a decision between leaving that place or sending hunters to exterminate the wolves. They did not want to be the kind of people who destroyed other creatures for their security and so they left that place. When the council gathered afterwards they decided that for every decision they made about their location or circumstance they would include Wolf Brother in the discussion. From that time onwards someone would ask: 'Who speaks for Wolf?'

It's a story I discovered a few years after meeting a wolf in the Canadian forest and every time I read it I'm moved. To know that there were (and are still) cultures in other lands which give so much respect to the wider community of life fills me with humility, and also with shame about my own. As I was researching the extinction of wolves in England and Wales and discovered the wolf hunter Peter Corbett, a Google search brought up a recent article in *Farmers Weekly* praising the acts of Corbett and extolling the virtues of a culture which seeks to protect its people by exterminating all potentially dangerous species. In the past two decades I've seen the same motivation used to exterminate many predators and carrion species, including foxes, badgers, hawks and crows. Our own culture seems unable to contain its own rapacious need to control everything.

After the poisoning of the River Llynfi, much attention was given to the state of local rivers. A citizen science movement grew and now frequently records contamination along the whole length of the Wye and some of its tributaries. Charities have been set up to raise awareness and combat the pollution, articles have appeared in local and national newspapers and the issue has been the subject of debates on radio and television. Recently Herefordshire Council made a request to the national government for permission to create a protected area and to control polluting farming and industry in the Wye catchment area. That permission was rejected by the Minister for Nature Recovery on the grounds that it would be more red tape for businesses, impeding their ability to compete. At the same time as this decision was made, due to an energy crisis governments worldwide were putting through legislation to drill for oil in places that have, up until now, been off limits, including in pristine areas of the oceans and rainforest. In Europe coal-fired power stations are coming back online and many projects to insulate houses and to install solar and wind energy have been postponed. As the journalist George Monbiot put it: 'It's as if they actively seek to destroy the living planet.'

A week ago the thermometer on the outside of my house read thirty-eight degrees for two days in a row, the highest temperature ever recorded in this area. Looking at the forecast we are due another thirty-degree-plus period next week. Wildfires are flaring up in the south of England where a drought has been ongoing for months. Roads and runways melted. Across the continent many areas are on fire, crops withering in the prolonged drought and vulnerable people dying. Every single community on Earth, human or wild, has now encountered losses caused by the depletion of nature and by global warming. Unless we find a way to heal the damage we've done the losses will accelerate. It will take a huge shift in our psyches to achieve this. Every country, city and village, every community and family, needs to ask the question: Who speaks for wolf, for bear, for fox, for gull, for heron, for kingfisher – for all species, not just our own?

*

Though it can take different forms the thought process of someone who is suffering from depression is dominated by the same question: What am I about to lose? It begins when your eyes open in the morning and does not stop repeating until you fall asleep at night. In my own case the question was urgent for a long period of time. I could have lost the love of my life. But Julia has recovered. She had a hysterectomy to prevent the potential spread of cancer into her womb and the tissue results post-operation came back clear. Medications which were making her sick have been replaced by gentler treatments and she is now well. Anxiety has a trigger, the more things that happen to cause it the more sensitive the trigger gets. For us, life has not returned to normal just yet. Every medical appointment is met with a wave of fear, every day when Julia feels

unwell creates a new tributary of worry. Hopefully, in time, this will subside. In the meantime we've acted to improve our lives. We've simplified, downsized and given ourselves as much time as we can. For me that meant quitting a job with a two-hour-each-way commute and a growing 24/7 industry culture. A period of exhaustion is now over and I'm devoting my expanded days to the wild. This book is the beginning of the work. I don't know, however, if the depression I feel will ever completely leave. My attachment to life has become more fierce in the past few years and that means accepting its wounds. Perhaps I should not see depression as an illness but as a symptom of the damage which reaches across the species barrier, into the hills, the rivers, every tributary and stream. The psychologist James Hillman once said that depression can be a natural and just response to a damaged environment, a sign that you're still sane.

We're spending more and more time near water. The narrowboat is Julia's happy place and the river has been a revelation to me, a place of riches. I witness many species of bird in the spring and summer. I spend hours kayaking, following the calls of cuckoos, seeing more in a day than I've seen in two decades in the uplands. The reeds are filled with warblers, grebes, coots and other nesting birds, and the meadows are frequented by sandpipers and curlews. It is estimated that there are twenty breeding pairs of curlews on the two-mile stretch I walk each day. I hear them constantly, from dawn to dusk. But the highlight for me are the common terns. I've only ever seen terns once before, a brief glimpse of a group of Arctic terns feeding in a loch on the Isle of Skye. A few days ago I sat in my kayak watching a pair move upriver, plunge-diving into the water to fish. They seem so fragile in the air, little strips of white cloth hanging from a puppeteer's strings. Then they fold themselves and spear down, cutting the surface into rings. A second later they're out and rowing almost vertically back over the trees. I watched them for half an hour as they continually fished around me. Later in the day they came to the narrowboats and began diving into the spaces between them, which are always filled with small fish.

Even in the cold months the place is filled with life. The gaps where the terns fish in summer becomes a place for kingfishers. They perch on the mooring ropes early in the morning and dive continually, sometimes within touching distance. Grey herons watch from the opposite bank. On the boat I become invisible to the inhabitants, part of the river, moving gently with it. Through those inhabitants I can see the wildness of the world and its kaleidoscopic transformations.

Herons have colonised many of the watery areas of the globe. They range through Africa, the Americas, Eurasia and Australia. Only the great tundras, sand and ice deserts, are empty of them. Globally sixty-seven species in the family exist. Their colours, forms and names are truly exotic: zigzag heron, cinnamon bittern, boat-billed heron, rufescent tiger heron, black-crowned night heron, lava heron, Pacific reef heron. Their tones graduate from jet black to ice white, their hues from teal, through deep burgundy, to lemon yellow. They can be seen on the edges of estuaries, riverbanks, streams, in rice fields, marshes, coral reefs, in the centre of villages, towns, cities, and in the remotest areas of rainforests. Kingfishers are even more multifarious than herons, with 114 species in the family inhabiting most of the globe. They are not all river birds, some are adapted to live in deserts, mountains and dense forests and they've existed there for almost forty million years. The smallest of them, the African dwarf kingfisher, is a minuscule bird only ten centimetres long; the biggest, the giant kingfisher, is five times that length; and the heaviest, the Australian laughing kookaburra, weighs half a kilogram. They are ringed, collared, crested, striped, pied. They are emerald green, bright jade, sky blue, neon pink. Ask a child to invent their own kingfisher with as many colours as they like and it probably already exists. These beings are connected over time and space to a quiet stretch of river where the narrowboats are moored, and to another river, just over the border into Wales, where their sibling species reside. To feel that connection I only need to read their names. My imagination will do the rest.

DUSK FALL

Dusk approaches. The horizon is an undulating line against which the silhouette of a single thorn tree billows up and leans away from the wind. An old farmer is driving a battered truck over the ruts he made decades ago. He's been told that one of his ewes is sick and lying in a ditch. The truck leans and skids over polished clay, pushes through clumps of sedge, edges past a pool, around it a halo of soft mud imprinted with hundreds of cloven hoofprints. He leans out of the window and shouts to his sheepdogs, which cross and recross the ground in front of him. He turns the truck north and spooks a snipe which has been sleeping in a clump of bracken. It shrieks its ghost call and he watches it zigzag away over the blue glint of the water. In a ditch he finds the stranded ewe, stops the truck and steps out. The sheep tries to escape, but it can only nod its head and scrabble its back legs weakly. The old man bends and lifts it to its feet, but a front leg is broken. He wheezes under the weight of it, struggles to open the back door of his truck and then manoeuvres the ewe inside. He shakes his head, curses, calls his dogs home.

A mile downhill water seeps through cracks in a pile of stones left only this morning by a little boy looking for the fossils of dinosaurs. In some of the stones he saw tiny shell-shaped indentations, little fans and spirals. He helped his father prise open layers in the soft rock, lifting slabs of it away from the edge of the stream bed. The slabs held the wave and ripple imprints of an estuary bed, frozen in time, buried for millions of years. The boy dropped them and watched them crack. Now the blue evening light catches on the ripple edges. A dipper has just arrived. It stands watching the stream, nodding, hungry after a lean day. The water is dim and the bird's eyes cannot pierce its surface to view the larvae, nymphs and minnows it feeds on. But it will wait patiently, stay until the last glints are gone and then find its roosting place, a gap in an old stone pillar that leans out from the bank.

The stream steps down, over faults in the rock, over weirs and fish ladders. It flows under lanes, through culverts, past abandoned mills, between the legs of cows, until it cuts through an almost sheer-sided gorge with ash, oak, hazel and holly growing over a rampant understorey of ferns and wildflowers. There are places here which have not been seen by a single living human, safe spaces for the fox, badger and otter, though always the sound of falling water is intermingled with the hiss of tyres and the clatter of farm machines. High in the boughs of a spindly tree which grasps the side of a stone outcrop, a goshawk is staring with fire eyes. There are a thousand people living nearby, but none of them have ever seen it, though this is the fifth year the bird has nested here. It waits, sitting on three pale eggs, feeling their warmth. The first of its young will hatch when the sun returns.

Below the tree the stream widens and slides down a ramp of stone, collects in a pool, then rides into a channel which flows out to the floodplain. Before it meets the river it crosses a flat expanse of farmland, planted with a monocrop of rapeseed, stretching like a blanket of sulphur along the valley floor. In a few weeks the crop will be harvested, processed and most of it burned as fuel. Now it holds the fading light in a single hue like a chemical stain. The stream enters the river, which, in this place, flows almost directly east to west. Downstream are the lowlands, upstream the mountains, and a thousand fast-flowing tributaries. The light turns the river into a tapering ribbon, glinting where the valley opens, falling into shadow where the woods and cliffs overhang. Next to a concrete bridge which rumbles with the wheels of cars a little egret is standing in the reeds, its shape like a sweep of calligraphy. It is a newcomer to this place, having crossed a sea, following a plume of warm air which does not normally reach so far north. It has brought with it the dazzling light of the south, which seems to have stuck to its feathers like burrs, even at twilight. A man watches it from above, leaning over the bridge railings, trying to capture an image of the bird with his phone. But the light is low and the image he captures is just a blur, an aura of the bird. As his dog pokes its head through a gap in the railings the egret twitches into life, spreads its wings and flees.

Where the river bends the bird rises above the trees and flies west, over fields of dozing cattle, over grey sheds, over a small town sprawled at the foot of a mountain. There it catches sight of another river and follows it, cutting over its twists and turns until a lake appears, glowing pewter to gold. The egret descends and lands on a tree-covered island. The lake is alive with birds, its surface intersected by house martins and sand martins which twist and swoop, glutting on a million swarming insects. Crested grebes, swans, Canada geese, teal and mallards cross the water serenely, bisecting each other's wakes. Close to the reeds coots and moorhens tussle and bob, trailed by their tiny, skittering young. The calls coming from the reeds are beginning to subside as the shade gathers. All day it has been a cacophony of cries from warblers, buntings and grebes, the birds invisible but clustered, gathered tight for the breeding season. This is the largest natural lake in the country, a stopping place for migrants, a protected space for resident birds, a rich food source and a breeding ground. Over two hundred species gather here over the year in the mosaic of habitats which surround the water. It always teems with life.

High above the island, where the egret has now stalked into the deep cover beneath hazel branches, a buzzard swings, hangs at the peak of its glide then slides back down the arc. It can see thin lines of colour in the west: saffron, goldenrod, persimmon. It can see every detail of the lake below, every hollow and wrinkle in the water, every insect and bird in pursuit, the surface like a slide beneath the lens of a microscope.

The lake is surrounded by a cauldron of mountains from which watersheds flow in every direction, ridges massed together, threaded with rivers and streams, spattered with oligotrophic pools. From high above, a buzzard's view, this landscape is creased and split like old paint. In the north-west a high plateau is ochred by the last daylight, its surface a tawny carpet of bitten grasses. It could be sand and rock, a thousand square miles of desert in the wettest of lands. In that place, as the light slides west, it will find no tree to silhouette against the sky, only piles of stones, fence posts and wire, signal towers, trig points. We've left our mark there in negative space, stripping away everything that grew more than a few centimetres from the ground. From every ridge top you can see 360 degrees of sky against which the bald-topped mountains rise, not in peaks, but in the curved shapes of ergs.

*

On a stone wall which keeps nothing out or in, a raven is perched. It seems to be waiting for something which is out of sight or hearing. It tilts its head to one side, then straightens. The tuft on its beak is bristled, its beard and feathers black ruffles, its eyes two perfect crystal balls containing cirrus clouds. It feels the trigger of the wind and leaps from the stones. It climbs high, then leans and glides out over a shallow valley, crossing a featureless basin. It climbs again, glides and climbs, then grates out a call which is answered by multiple croaks, coming from every direction. There are specks of blue-black moving against the wind. The raven speeds up, climbs higher, crosses another summit and reaches a shatter of rock, the top of a cliff which drops sheer into a gorge. All day the rock has been warming and now the wind is coming against it, channelling the air into a high plume. Other birds are arriving, sliding into the thermal, riding it vertically then turning, hanging for a moment, before folding their wings and clattering down. The raven meets them, calling out as it catches the tower of air, and rides. It is a dance and an airborne circus, a comic act at half-light. The birds pair up and fly in duets. They beat their wings in time, plummet almost to the valley floor, then rise. As they catapult out they flip and twist. They grab each others talons, peck and yawn, screech with corvid laughter. The act continues, each aerobatic turn different to the last, more precarious, more chaotic.

*

West of the cliff where the ravens dive there is an area of land cleanly cut into almost perfect rectangles which now glow green and grey. In the middle of this space are several buildings big enough to house a passenger jet. Inside each are forty thousand unfledged chickens, crammed together. The birds are bathed in light coming from lamps hanging from the ceiling, set to create a timed day and night. Trays of food and water filled mechanically run in lines across the floor. The birds gorge on the feed, putting on weight rapidly, each of them engineered genetically for this. A man is moving among them, carrying a net. He walks slowly, looking for birds which are struggling to walk or stand. Some have tumours, or crippled legs, heart or lung disease. When he spots one he picks it up, snaps its neck against the feeder bar and throws it, still twitching, into a bin. He does this up to five hundred times each day in each barn. Sometimes his technique isn't right and a bird will be thrown alive into the bin to slowly suffocate, crushed by other bodies. The operation needs to make sure each bird grows in the shortest period of time, it's the difference between profit and loss. The hangar floor is covered in faeces which is dug out at intervals and spread on the surrounding land. The rains come and the dung leaches into the streams, then passes into the rivers, which turn green, choking and poisoning aquatic life.

When the birds hit target weight they are piled into crates, driven to factories, slaughtered, processed and sent to the clean white shelves of supermarkets. We buy three million of them every day. Outside the shed it is quiet, the low whirr of the air scrubbers, housed in each roof, overlaying the engine growl of an articulated truck which has just pulled into the yard to take the next load for processing. As the engine dies the sound of distant ravens overlays the quiet, a cackling response to the dark comedy of life.

*

The light has faded further and though there is still an hour to go before dark, every creature has felt its coming. Down the valley, just out of sight of the chicken sheds, a young girl is walking across a field deep in buttercups. She rips some of them from the ground,

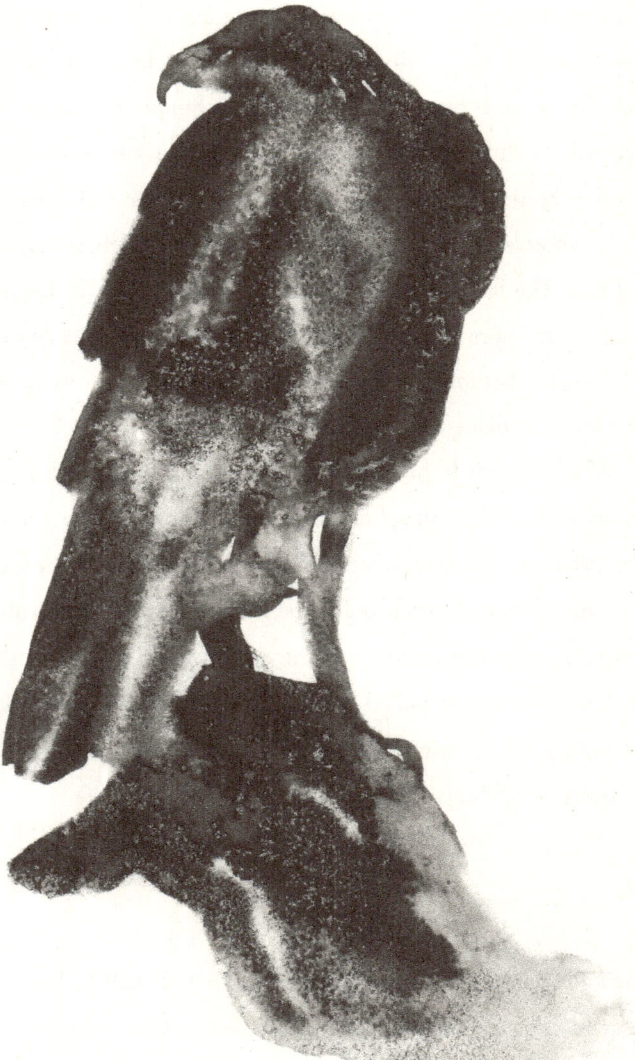

plucks at their petals, sniffs them, licks them to discover their taste. As she does so she drops the head collars she has been carrying and stops to pick them up. The horses are in the far corner of the field, ripping at the new grass, which has taken longer this year to come. She watches them for a moment, then calls their names softly. Their ears turn to catch her voice, but the horses do not move. As she comes closer her grey pony rears, spooks and clatters away. Her old companion horse, which hasn't galloped all year, follows the pony at full speed. She calls them again as they turn and race towards her, running side by side. They pass her at full speed and circle back. When they reach the middle of the field they come to a halt and start to graze peacefully, as if nothing had happened.

Two swallows are crossing the field so low they could sip from the mouths of the flowers. They arrived only a few days ago, late this year, and are now furiously feeding, following each other, swooping around the horses. Their nest is in the stable. The girl has been mixing earth and old hay with water from the trough, making cakes of mud which she piled at the gate, helping them to renovate their nests in preparation for this year's broods, three last year, perhaps only two this time. The horses run from her again, wild and uncatchable. She will give up and leave them, chase the swallows instead. Her grandfather watches from the stable. He has seen the swallows return over seventy times and remembers when there were so many of them they used to fly through the upstairs windows, in one side of the house, down the stairs and out the other. There were peewits nesting in his fields then, and curlews.

He tries to remember when he last saw either, and if there have ever been so few swallows.

*

A single-track road passes the farm and climbs steeply to a plateau which is almost lifeless, even at this high point of the year. What creatures there are here seem like fugitives, so spread apart, as if isolation has been forced on them. To the west there is a line of rock which rises vertically. The soft, layered stone is wind-carved into tall, leaning chimneys too fragile to climb. There are mossy, inaccessible ledges with thin trees growing out of them. A crow has nested in the tangled branches of a spindly rowan. It sits in the cup of the nest now, staring out at the bare land. Behind it there is a fissure in the cliff, invisible from below. It has been partially blocked for centuries by a boulder fall, but behind it is a cave the size of a large room. On the floor are five human skeletons. Around them, placed into alcoves and recesses in the rock, are the remains of the tools they used: flint fragments, pot shards. Scattered among these are the bones of goats, horses, badgers, wild boars, bears. There are many animal teeth, some of them drilled with holes through which a string was once threaded. Some of the larger bones have decorative marks scratched into them, lines and cross-hatches, rough circles. In this dark place is a world long extinct. There are caves and chambers like this all over Wales. Some are filled with our burial goods, others with the bones of cohabitants: cave bears, lions, wolves. In other places are rarer finds, bone fragments of rhinos and straight-tusked elephants, their remains a reminder that this land has transformed so many times, and will transform again.

Outside the cave there is a flurry of wings and the crow screeches. A tiercel peregrine has just landed on a higher ledge. It is hungry. It has flown from a high cliff above a reservoir where it has been hunting unsuccessfully for days. It has been attacked by rooks, ravens, other crows. A snapped leather leash hangs from one foot. The falcon bites at it. It escaped its keeper a week ago on the high moor to the south and has remained in this place of hunger. It will not survive if it stays. Soon the crow's mate will return and the pair will harass the falcon. Though they are not as fast and strong they are smarter, more tenacious, with young to protect. The falcon will be seen off, leaving a single barred feather on the ledge outside the cave. It will fly west, climbing so high it will see the blue line of the ocean. Then it will see a steeple rising like a spear point out of the land and roost there tonight.

The church is on the edge of a scattered village, depopulated now. It has not been used for decades. There are many slates missing on the roof, and some of the windows are smashed. Inside, the pews are stacked in a corner, blackened by layers of mould. There are old books rotting in piles, plastic sacks filled with debris. The plaster on the walls has fallen away and the floor is cracked, open to the clay beneath. Pigeons have roosted in here for years, jackdaws have built their nests. The place is covered with their droppings. Spores and seeds have found their way in, blown by the wind or dropped by birds. An interior garden is beginning to grow, hart's tongue ferns and lady ferns fanning from the cracks in the floor, an ash sapling struggling into life below a window. Bats are waking in the spaces above. Two are circling over the pews. In minutes they will be outside, hunting in the overgrown graveyard, above and beneath the yews.

The church gate leads on to a narrow lane deeply carved into the hillside, following the old pilgrims' route west to the edge of the sea. It climbs steeply for a mile through dense hazel woods, then disappears into pasture and ploughed fields. Two brothers are preparing to camp for the night on the edge of a field. They have walked twenty miles every day for a week, from their home east of the border. They have just lost their mother to cancer and they are carrying her ashes to the sea at St David's. Other pilgrims still pass this way, some attempting to follow the ways of the saints, others to take in the landscape, to beat illness, to remember. Along the path they will see the remains of the old travellers, steps worn into rocks, carved crosses and waymarks. Though they are taking the same route they are crossing a country which bears little resemblance to the one the old pilgrims travelled through. Most of its wild inhabitants are gone.

*

Above the field where the brothers are camping the light has intensified, reflected by the sea, which is only a few miles away. Here the upland gives way to green valleys over which solitary crags and rocky outcrops stand. The terrain follows the arc of Cardigan Bay, the western edge of Wales. Roughly in its centre and set back from the sea's edge is another large complex of hangar-like buildings. A gallery hall in this concrete structure is now locked. Its high walls have no windows, the only light seeping into the room coming from the glass panel doors, which project two pale rectangles on to the polished floor. Occasionally someone passes in the corridor outside, soft footsteps, lowered voices, as if respecting the dead. The rest of the time the hall is in total silence. A large white plinth hovers above the floor. On it is a crystal skeleton, laid out perfectly, every bone symmetrical to its opposite: ribs, mandibles, humeri, ulnas. The assemblage is six metres long, the skeleton of a minke whale. It was washed up dead on a beach on the other side of the UK, a place facing the North Sea. Its organs, skin and flesh were stripped, the skeleton cleaned. Each bone was then immersed in a concentrated alum solution which produced an outgrowth of crystals encrusting the surface like frost. It is the work of the artists Ackroyd and Harvey, titled *Stranded*, a reflection of the processes of ocean acidification, of climate change and the loss of whale species. The work is perhaps at its most powerful now, locked in the silent hall with no one to witness it, the crystals clinging to the sliver of light penetrating the room. In an hour the lights in the building will go off. The whale will disappear, back to the depths of the ocean. All over the world there are rooms like this, some as big as barns, others tiny, the interiors of boxes and drawers. In them are hosts of species, carefully catalogued and chemically preserved, or reconstructed from remains. They are homes to creatures from every part of the planet and from every era of Earth's long history. Some reside in the rooms of children, or hobby collectors, others in schools and colleges, in museums and galleries. Many house examples of extinct species, or those which will soon become extinct.

*

At the far western tip of the bay the last tooth of the upland reaches out towards the sea. A ridge, shaped like the back of a giant lizard, perches at St David's Head, overlooking a three-toed peninsula, the most westerly point in Wales, our *finis terrae*. Above the hill are the wheeling shapes of herring gulls, greater and lesser black backs, more than a hundred of them, silhouetted against a sky which is beginning to blend with the sea. Their harsh calls mix with the hiss of wind and waves. Among the piled rocks there are signs of old settlements, a burial chamber, enclosure walls, the remains of house platforms. For thousands of years we have occupied these isles to their very edges.

A few miles south Skomer is a sprawl of ancient field walls, hill forts, chambered tombs. On its north side is a scar in the cliff where a ramp was cut to transport livestock on to the island centuries ago, sheep and cattle made to swim across the sound from the mainland. Its abandoned fields are now a warren covered with a million bluebells. We have withdrawn, but only a fraction. Though the island is no longer farmed it is still under our control, a place for tourism and research. We monitor the resident and migrant species, counting their numbers, observing their declines, making and revising best guesses about causes.

*

There is only the faintest glow in the west. Colours are gone. Against the horizon one shape is just visible, a molar of rock, paler than the sky, as if a weak lamp lights it. Across the water another pale shape is moving, faint enough to be an afterglow. The bird is flying west, its wings beating fast, as if it were trying to catch up with the light. The sulphur yellow of its head and neck feathers is not visible and the black tips of its wings have disappeared. It could be a gull, a tern, a swan or the ghost of a bird. The gannet is heading to the little rock far out at sea where thousands of its kind are sitting on eggs or warming newly hatched chicks. For the coming months the island will be alive with their calls, with their whiteness and stink, the colony like a single organism spread across the rock. The last light of dusk will fade away in a gannet's wild eye.

ACKNOWLEDGEMENTS

I would like to thank the team at September for their help and support in the making of this book, particularly Hannah MacDonald for her encouragement, faith in my work and ongoing editorial feedback. Also, thanks to Jo Walker for adapting my illustrations and creating such a beautiful cover design. I am also grateful to my agent Robert Caskie for helping to steer the process, which I am so new to.

Two Lights evolved from my essay 'Chorus', which was originally published by Little Toller Press. My thanks to them for making the work visible, and for their support.

I would like to express my appreciation to a group of poets, writers and editors who have supported my work consistently over many years. Without them a book would not have emerged. Thanks to Patricia McCarthy, Jane Lovell, Tanya Shadrick and Sharon Blackie.

Thank you to the wolf and the curlews, who asked the questions.

Above all thank you to Julia, who, while slowly recovering from a long illness, found the energy to take on the role of co-conspirator.